MORE SERMONS FR

MORE SERMONS FROM GREAT ST. MARY'S

Edited by
HUGH MONTEFIORE

HODDER AND STOUGHTON
LONDON SYDNEY AUCKLAND TORONTO

FOREWORD

These addresses are selected from courses held at Great St. Mary's during the final three years of my ministry at the University Church. The enthusiastic response to the earlier volume, *Sermons from Great St. Mary's*, has encouraged me to edit this second volume.

Once again it has been exceedingly difficult to select from the galaxy of preachers those addresses that ought to be included here. I have tried to proceed on the same lines as before, except that there is a wider range of speakers, with a large representation of laymen covering literature, music, science, medicine and law. There is also a significant contribution from an agnostic to show how much Christians and humanists can co-operate in practical matters: other addresses show up very clearly the differences between them. Readers may think that the unscripted discussions are among the more valuable contributions.

There are, of course, significant omissions. Some superb sermons could not be included because they are already being published elsewhere; in particular a course of three addresses by the Archbishop of Canterbury. Once again there are few addresses on ethical themes. This is because a series in this field is included in a recent collection of mine published under the title *Can Man Survive?* It gives me particular pleasure to have been able to include an address by my successor, Stanley Booth-Clibborn, given before he became Vicar of Great St. Mary's.

I still believe in the great value of the printed sermon. I hope that readers will find them as compulsive reading as I found them compulsive listening.

HUGH MONTEFIORE

August 1970

ACKNOWLEDGMENT

'Final Instructions' by C. Day Lewis is reproduced from *Pegasus* by permission of Jonathan Cape Ltd.

CONTENTS

FUNDAMENTAL QUESTIONS

ON CHRISTIANITY

ARTS, SCIENCES AND LAW

AFRICA AND ENGLAND

THE CHRISTIAN LIFE

FUNDAMENTAL QUESTIONS

CHAPTER ONE

CHRIST OUR LORD—OR WHO?

by the Archbishop of York,
The Most Reverend DONALD COGGAN, D.D.

If we are to consider the person of Christ we've got to begin with the documents. This means that if we are to tackle the theme in an intellectually respectable fashion we've got to start with the New Testament: and here I see two stages, and then beyond that I shall touch on a third stage. The people round our Lord when he trod the highways and by-ways of Galilee and Samaria and Judaea were naturally enough, like him, Jews; a race pretty sharply distinguished from their neighbours. That was one reason why they were so unpopular, as indeed in many parts of the world today they still are. People couldn't understand why, for example, they wouldn't eat any pork, or why they refused to work on the seventh day (they would rather die than do that), or why their girls wouldn't marry Gentile boys or vice versa, why they concentrated so much on their closely knit family life, why they made so much of their local synagogue. (This was the place where justice was dispensed and education was given and every seventh day there was regular worship and the reading of the law, in fact the very centre of their life wherever there was a decent-sized community.) Their neighbours couldn't understand why they made such a fuss about the feasts to which, whenever they could, they went up to Jerusalem in parties. They kept to themselves and that gave rise to misunderstanding. But what they stood for above all else was the doctrine which is summed up in the belief that there is one God and one God alone.

This great doctrine of monotheism cries out from almost every page of the Old Testament. It is taken up by our Lord in his teaching, and it is epitomised in the 'Hear O Israel', the great *Shema* as they call it. 'Hear O Israel, the Lord our God is one Lord.' This is our Lord's preface, taken straight out of the Old Testament, to the twofold command to love God and to love our neighbour. They used some pretty tough language about the nation if it departed from that belief. If Israel played false to that central theme of monotheism, then the prophets used to say that Israel had committed adultery against its God. It was strong language because they dared to speak of Jahweh their God as the husband of his people and of the people as the bride of their God. This is daring language, but it served to under-line how terrible they thought anything was that might infringe on the doctrine of monotheism. When a Jew prayed he saw the God of Abraham, Isaac and Jacob, the God of the Israelite people, the God who had led them down the paths of their history. Men and women died in vast numbers for this belief in the one true God. If you've never read the Books of the Maccabees—I Maccabees especially—get hold of an Apocrypha. Read the first few chapters of I Macca-bees. They are bloody chapters because they tell the story of a fellow called Antiochus Epiphanes which meant 'God made manifest'—not a bad title for a king, but his enemies called him Epimanes which meant 'mad-hatter'. They tell the story of how this man tried to bring these people to heel; but they weren't having any syncretism. They would stand by this great central doctrine. They did, and they died, died in great numbers; they were wiped out because they were faithful to that belief. And if you think they were narrow-minded, just ask yourself whether you've got any belief dear enough for you to die for. Many of us haven't got enough belief to live by!

That is a simple bit of history. The point I'm coming to is this: that within a very short time of the death and resurrection of Jesus, Jews, strong monotheistic Jews, are found praying to him. Now this seems to me intensely sig-nificant. Let me give you an example. If you turn to the Acts of the Apostles, the first bit of history of the Christian Church, at the end of the seventh chapter you'll get the story of the death by stoning of the proto-martyr of the Christian Church, Stephen. It was a fearful, ugly death; not as bad as crucifixion but often long-drawn-out and awful. As his end draws near, he prays. Jesus as his end drew near, had said, 'Father, into thy hands I commend my spirit.' Stephen's prayer was very similar and very different, 'Receive my spirit,' he says. But to whom does he address his prayer? It was 'Lord Jesus, receive my spirit'. So it went on. Christolatry preceded christology, prayer came before the defining of doctrine with any nicety. When these early Christians knelt or stood to say their prayers, they saw the face of Jesus. As they prayed and looked back and looked up, they couldn't simply say, 'Oh he was a good man.' That wasn't adequate. Somehow the twelve apostles and he didn't make thirteen. There was that about him that was so unique that they didn't simply say 'He was'. They said 'He is'. He was so real that they addressed their prayers to him and that, I repeat, seems deeply significant.

Call that Stage One if you will. If you're wise in thinking out the question in the title of our sermon tonight, you'll ponder long and hard on that.

For our second stage we turn to the Gospels, and especially to our Lord's language about himself, so far as we can gather it. It seems to me that four things stand out reasonably clearly. He seems to have claimed, first, a unique oneness with God, so much so that he incurred from his critics the charge of blasphemy. He had a unique relationship with God. Then, secondly, he seems to have claimed a moral authority over men. St. Mark, the earliest of the four Gospels, makes a great point of this. Right at the beginning of the story, when Jesus came and started teaching, men said, 'What is this? A new teaching,' and Mark comments, 'He taught with authority.' Yet it wasn't as the scribes taught. They were the people who had the traditional authority, but this was something new. And his teaching was so often self-directed. This is the last thing that any ordinary Christian teacher ought to do. One's great prayer when you preach a sermon is to forget about yourself and think about the God of whom you're preaching. But our Lord constantly directed attention to himself, and his great imperious invitation 'Follow me' implies moral authority over men. Then he seems to have claimed a unique ministry of salvation to men. 'The Son of Man came not to be ministered to but to minister and to give his life a ransom for the many.' I mustn't start on that saying with all its Old Testament nuances; but it was a ministry of salvation to men. Fourthly, he seems to have claimed a unique mastery over the powers of evil.

These four things that stand out in the first three Gospels are in a way admirably summed up in the prologue to the

Fourth Gospel where St. John chose the word *logos* out of many which he might have used to describe this One who had invaded this world as God's messenger. When he used the description 'the Word' to describe our Lord, he used a term that was understood both by the Jews and by the Gentiles. The Greeks thought of *logos* as reason, the Jews thought of it as the creative power of God, God in action among men. When St. John said, 'In the beginning was the Word, and the Word was made flesh and tented among us,' it was his way of saying, 'If you want to hear what God has to say to us men, then look at Jesus, listen to Jesus, obey the word of Jesus. He is what God has to say to men.' This I suppose is the supreme passage of the New Testament. But it isn't by any means unique. This is the only passage where Jesus is specifically spoken of as the *logos* of God, the Word of God. But you get very close to it in other strata of your New Testament evidence. In a superb passage at the beginning of the Epistle to the Hebrews come these words: 'God who at different times and in diverse manner spake to the Fathers by the prophets, has in these last days spoken to us *en huio*, in one who has the characteristic of Son.' He doesn't call him the Word but he's saying much the same thing; and the Epistle to the Colossians has 'the image of the invisible God'—this is how he describes Jesus Christ within a comparatively few years of his appearance among us: 'By Him creation came into being, through Him all things cohere.' This runs like a major theme through the main documents of the New Testament. Then you get from time to time what I might call trinitarian hints, long before the councils of the Church got going with their definitions. 'By Him,' says the writer of the Epistle to the Ephesians referring to our Lord, 'by Him we both have access by one Spirit to the Father.' And in the great prayer we used tonight, 'The grace of our Lord Jesus Christ, the love of God, and the fellowship of the Holy Spirit,' you've got as it were the beginning of a trinitarian doctrine. You can almost watch the evolution of a philosophy of history building up with Christ as its centre. That's the second stage.

Then, as it were in the distance, you begin to see a third stage, the formulation of the Creeds, when on the anvil of the early heresies the doctrines of christology were hammered out: 'God from God, Light from Light, Very God from Very God.' The language of the old councils needs constant reinterpretation. We can't just leave them like that. But what I want you to remember tonight is this. The beginning of all this formulation was not a tableful of theologians wanting to think out something clever but a group of men and women of all kinds of background and experience who were faced by certain realities which beg for some kind of formulation. Through their contact directly or at one or two removes with Jesus Christ they had come into touch with the forgiving love of God that they called grace. In a unique way 'the grace of our Lord Jesus Christ' was a reality the like of which they had seen in no one before. The love of God, which before perhaps had been something of a theory to them, came flooding in since their contact with Christ, and this fellowship of the Holy Spirit of Jesus, this togetherness which the spirit of Jesus had created when he was on earth and which continued at a deeper and wider level when his bodily presence was withdrawn, this was a reality the like of which they had never dreamed before their contact with him. Grace, love, fellowship were all linked with Jesus. It was these tremendous experiences of realities hitherto unknown that cried out for some kind of expression and which gave birth eventually to the Creeds.

I want to suggest to you that along those three lines you might work away at your title for tonight if—as I believe you do from the way you're listening—you want to think hard about it: 'Christ Our Lord or Who?'

I want now, against that threefold background, to make a comment and to ask a question. The comment is this. When we're dealing with the person of Christ we're necessarily dealing with a matter of faith rather than of knowledge only. There is, I believe, a good basis of fact to what we've been considering, but like many of the greatest things in life, this cannot be proved like so many mathematical propositions. I can't prove, just like that, that my wife loves me. She's put up with me for thirty-three years and that, I should think, takes a great deal of love. There are evidences that she does. You haven't got a kind of mathematical proof that your fiancée or your mother or your father loves you, but you've enough to bet on, you've enough to found a decision on, to base your life on, enough to prove it as you go along.

What a moving lesson that was that was read to us tonight from St. John's Gospel! Thomas, the first of the two about whom we heard, had heard the claims of Jesus, he had pondered them, he had weighed them up. Then he was faced with this ghastly contradiction, this terrible crucifixion, this blotting out, as he thought, of that to which he was pinning his faith. He was shaken to the roots of his being. And then he heard the voice of Jesus say to him, 'Thomas, don't become an unbeliever' (I think that's how the Greek ought to be translated, *me ginou apistos*). 'Don't become an unbeliever, that's where you're going if you aren't awfully careful, but that is disaster. Thomas, don't! stop it! don't become an unbeliever.' At that point Thomas fell down and worshipped; he adored: 'My Lord, my God.'

And now for the question.

Somebody may say, 'Does it really matter very much anyway? All this business about the person of Christ, who he is and what we do about him, isn't it all much ado about, well not nothing, but something not terribly important?' I would answer that with the deepest conviction, 'I believe it matters intensely.' What you think and what you decide about the person and the claims of Jesus are crucial questions. You'd be very wise in your university course, at whatever stage you are, if you call a halt until you've done some hard thinking and deciding about that. There's a passage in the Synoptic Gospels where our Lord is in converse with his disciples and they are having a gay time discussing who he was. He asks them what people are saying about him, and some say this and some say that, for he was the centre of great controversy and great differences of opinion. It was great fun to discuss him like that, as it were, at arms' length, academically, remotely. And then to their great discomfort, I imagine, Jesus turned and looked them in the eye. 'You, you, you, who do you say I am?' Ah! that's a very different matter, and Peter came out with his tremendous affirmation: 'The Christ of God.' But if you make that affirmation, then you've got to work it out. The experience of multitudes down the years has been that you find the truth about Christ as you begin to follow Christ. There was the story of the healing of the lepers. It was as they went that they were healed. It's as you follow that your doubts begin to go; and I thought the second bit of the lesson read to us tonight was deeply significant here. Here was Simon Peter, shaken again to his roots as Thomas had been. But Jesus asked him one question, he gave him one test. The question was, 'Do you love me?' and the test was 'Will you work for me? —because, Simon, as you work for me you'll find your faith.'

I culled this from John Whale the other day: 'After all there is a view from Helvellyn which only those on Striding Edge may see.' I won't apply that: you see the point. I didn't choose the title, but I think this is where the title of our sermon tonight is so significant: 'Christ our Lord' brings this discussion out of the realm of ancient history into the sphere of personal decision. I'm not concerned now about Stephen's Lord—I was earlier on—or Thomas's Lord or Peter's Lord, but *our* Lord, *my* Lord. And, annoyingly perhaps because it comes home so close, this title faces us with a choice—'Or who?' It implies, if I understand it rightly, that you've got to have a boss of one kind or another. If Jesus Christ isn't the Lord of your life someone else will be. You may think it will be yourself, you'll paddle your own canoe. 'I'm the master of my fate, I'm the captain of my soul,' as Henley put it in a memorable couplet. But what a disastrous mess we make it when we go it alone! Just this last week, I had to spend the best part of an hour and a half with a man who had made an utter mess of his life, because the domination of Christ had ceased to be a reality to him. In this hymn to Jesus, Morrison got much closer than Henley did:

> Make me a captive, Lord,
> And then I shall be free;
> Force me to render up my sword,
> And I shall conqueror be.

There's only one word there I can't take and that's the word force, for this is the one thing our Lord will never do. Augustine knew better than Morrison. Augustine said, 'God asks our leave to bless us.' That's right, God will never force us. He'll stand at the door and knock but never force the lock. But the point that Morrison is making is this. You must have a master and the only master worth total following is Jesus Christ. I believe that. I've seen it work out in the experience of so many.

They tell the story of a sculptor who did a great statue

of Jesus and it was greatly admired. People stood and looked at the lineaments so clean and strong and they walked round and admired it from this angle and that; but the sculptor said, 'If you want to see it in its right proportion you'd best kneel.' That's the only way you ever see Jesus, when like Thomas you fall at his feet and you say, 'My Lord and my God.' My faith may be tiny as a grain of mustard seed and my love, unlike Simon Peter's, perhaps so small that I'd hardly dare call that little flickering flame love at all; but 'Thou knowest, Lord'. When you kneel at his feet, you begin to see his proportions and you see, and you lay hold, and you live, and you find there's something in the lines of Myers with which I'm going to close. They are the lines with which he closes his poem on St. Paul. They've stuck in my mind and I'd like them to be a pointer to you:

Yea thro' life, death, thro' sorrow and thro' sinning,
He shall suffice me, for he hath sufficed:
Christ is the end, for Christ was the beginning,
Christ the beginning, for the end is Christ.

CHAPTER TWO

WHAT IS THE RESURRECTION?

An unscripted discussion between
Bishop JOHN ROBINSON and Bishop HUGH MONTEFIORE

H.M.: The title is 'What is the resurrection?' I think we ought to start off with what it means to us, how central it is to our faith today—the resurrection as a present event in experience. Would you like to say anything about that?

J.R.: Yes, I too would like to start there because I have found through experience that when I'm asked questions about the resurrection, I have to spend two or three minutes clearing up that the resurrection is not simply the empty tomb, which I think ninety per cent of people assume that it is. In that splendid lesson we have just heard from 1 Corinthians 15 you probably did not notice that Paul never once mentions the empty tomb. I suspect that he did probably believe it, but he never mentions it. It is simply not what he means by the resurrection, nor for that matter, are the appearances (which he lists in great detail), though that was how the belief got off the ground. What he means by the resurrection, when for example he is preaching 'Jesus and the resurrection' as the centre of everything in the Acts and when in the Epistles he speaks of 'the power of his resurrection'—this is something which can only be demonstrated by present and not by past evidence. It is essentially a spiritual reality which he feels has captured him and in which his whole life is now lived. It has transformed existence so that Jesus for him is no longer just a memory of a man who lived in the past but a present dynamic reality in the community of his followers. This is something which all Christians ever since have held and to which they have testified; and the vast majority of Christians, of course, have believed in the resurrection without any evidence either of the empty tomb or of the appearances but simply because they are convinced by something which 'gets' them.

H.M.: Could we expand on your last phrase 'something which gets them' because I think that many people feel that they haven't had a personal confrontation with someone who is still alive and therefore the resurrection isn't a real experience for them. For them the resurrection just means that someone is alive after being dead. But this really isn't the Christian experience at all. It's rather being lifted up through Christ into a new sort of life, and having felt his power in one's life. Will you agree here?

J.R.: Yes, and it's what the New Testament speaks of as 'Christ according to the Spirit'. In other words one is not dealing with simply an individual one might confront as I'm confronting you but with something that pervades one's whole being and is essentially corporate. To be 'in Christ' is to be in the community of those who accept this life and are transformed by it.

H.M.: Yes. Now that we have analysed what resurrection means in the present, a lot of people would like us to discuss 'What *was* the resurrection?' And I suppose the first question which we ought to think about is whether the resurrection led to the Christian faith or whether the Christian faith led to belief in the resurrection. There are those who say that the resurrection is a kind of 'putting into words' the feelings which early Christians had about Jesus. Do you agree?

J.R.: Well, certainly, there's no doubt whatever from that passage of St. Paul that has just been read that he saw the resurrection as absolutely crucial to the creation of the faith rather than the other way round; and the idea that the resurrection was somehow created by wishful thinking or feeling or hoping among the disciples seems to me to be psychologically just not a starter. It seems to be the last thing that they were expecting. Something got them, something transformed them which was quite contrary to all their expectations and turned them inside out. And unless there had been this real objective reality I can't see that the Easter faith would have come about at all.

H.M.: I must say that I'm in total agreement with you there. I don't think there is any matter for discussion between us. I'm puzzled that intelligent people do make such statements

and there must be reasons for them which I can't compre-
hend. So far as I understand, say, the psychology of bereavement, it seems to me to be against all expectation that the
faith could have given rise to the resurrection. It seems to
me that the only logical explanation is the other way round.
However, let us move on from that and ask ourselves to
what extent the resurrection of Jesus was different for the
early church, from, say, the raising to life of Lazarus. After
all, the story of Lazarus is that he was raised from the dead.
Whatever interpretation we put on St. John's Gospel, this
is the story. Now, after three days Jesus rose again from
the dead. What difference do you see between these two
events?

J.R.: Well, it's interesting I think that the New Testament
never uses the noun 'the resurrection' of anyone except Jesus.
It records other raisings from the dead—Jairus's daughter,
Lazarus and so on—but these are essentially in the area of
what we might call resuscitations. In other words they were
brought back to live the life they had been living, and pre-
sumably died again one day. Now this seems to me to be
quite different from what the early Christians were asserting of Christ, and by using the term 'the resurrection' of
him and of none of the others, what they were saying is that
in this event they saw, if you like, the beginning of the
end, because the term 'the resurrection' in Judaism had
never meant anything else up till that moment. The resurrection was something that was still going to happen at the
last day. The word is used like this in the Gospels for
instance: 'At the resurrection whose wife shall she be?' In
other words, at the end of the world people would be raised
in order to be judged. Now by asserting that the resurrection
was something which took place within history, on the third
day rather than on the last day, the New Testament writers
were in fact asserting something quite fundamental—that a
new age had dawned, the messianic era had begun. All these
other raisings to life may be seen as anticipations or 'signs
before the time' of the kind of power that is released in
Jesus. And so the Gospel writers see them, particularly I
think, St. John; but they never confuse the two.

H.M.: How would you say the early Church viewed the
relationship between something like that which we know

by the resurrection and that which we symbolise by the words 'the ascension'—which of course, is not a New Testament word as such. Do you think that the early Church made any great distinction between the two? Except in St. Luke's writings I can't see any myself.

J.R.: No, I don't think they did. Indeed except in Acts I can't see any, because even in his Gospel St. Luke probably saw the ascension taking place on Easter Day.

H.M.: Yes.

J.R.: It is only in Acts you get this forty-day period. And I think that what you get in Acts is, if you like, a sort of beginning of the 'Christian Year'. Here is an enormous complex which theologically is all one; there is the resurrection, there is the ascension, and the giving of the spirit—all these are aspects of the same event. And indeed in St. John they all take place on Easter Day, and I think it is the same in every other strand of the Gospel material. What Luke does is to space these out because, as though you can't take them all in in one day. Let us, he says, attach them to different festivals. And so you get them pegged out—after three days, forty days, fifty days. This is as a teaching method extremely valuable, but ultimately all the ascension means is that Jesus is not merely living but Lord; and this is just another aspect of the same Easter proclamation.

H.M.: I think we should move on to the reasons why we believe in the resurrection. We said that we didn't see that we could find any proper reason for the existence of the Church, unless something happened, something which 'got them' happened. Now we haven't any witness of the resurrection itself, not until a late and Apocryphal Gospel. There is no suggestion that anyone saw an event called the resurrection. What about the other witnesses—witnesses to the risen Lord? What witnesses have we got?

J.R.: Well, as you say, no one saw the resurrection. The first evidence of a new state of affairs came to the disciples in certain ways which we might today explain as psychic experiences. In other words they saw something, they had some kind of vision, some kind of visual experience of Christ as being alive. Now on what these appearances were, how physical they were, how psychological they were, there is a great deal of divergence in the New Testament accounts. The earliest account is undoubtedly that of St. Paul which was read just now, and he of course links the appearances to the other disciples with the appearance to himself on the Damascus Road and he sees them all as part of the same series. And both St. Paul himself and the author of Acts clearly visualise this appearance as being not primarily physical but something, as it were, which he saw as a spiritual vision, but which was no less objective for that. After all, it stopped him dead in his tracks and turned his whole life round. It certainly wasn't something that he imagined or that was purely hallucinatory in the sense of seeing pink rats. But nevertheless it obviously wasn't tangible and he visualised, I imagine, the appearances to other people as being roughly of the same sort. Indeed, I think that, however they describe the appearances, all the Gospel writers see them as appearances of the glorified Christ, especially the Fourth Gospel. St. John has some very physical appearances but nevertheless this is the moment when Jesus has been glorified and it is not the flesh-body which they see but some kind of transformed spiritual reality.

H.M.: I think we ought to face the fact that people are bound to say, 'This is the most extraordinary belief.' People said this on the Areopagus and people have been saying it ever since. 'This is an almost incredible belief. Produce your evidence!' And when we look at the Gospels, we don't find anything in St. Mark: there's no appearance in St. Mark at all. We find appearances in St. Matthew, in St. Luke and in St. John; and none of those are exactly the same—there are different localities, different events, almost different types of body. I mean, on one occasion we are told that Jesus ate something and on another occasion we are told he went through a door. What are we to make of these differences? We surely must give some intelligible account of how these differences came about, whether they were theologically motivated, whether there was some other reason—apologetic or otherwise—for the developing tradition and what light these accounts shed on what the original events were. For we are concerned with events, whether Jesus really did appear. Now, what would you say to that? What do you say about the divergences of evidence here, because they are considerable and they do need serious consideration. Are there any criteria, for example, by which we might distinguish a more primitive description of an appearance from another?

J.R.: I think it's very difficult to be dogmatic over this. Obviously one can give priority to St. Paul here, and within the Gospel tradition one can perhaps see a development in the direction of making these appearances more physical and more materialistic. I would not even be very dogmatic on that, frankly. What it does seem to me is that we've got considerable diversity, but I wouldn't say at any point radical contradiction. There is a great diversity of reporting, in much the same way as one gets in any account of psychic experiences. Now these are almost impossible to pin down, as one knows; and the fact that they happened in different places doesn't seem to me to be literally here or there because, if they were of this kind, then materialisations could take place in any different part of the globe even, and so the difference between Galilee and Jerusalem is just nothing. To that extent I don't see any real problem. I think clearly there are apologetic interests, I think Luke has some and possibly John. But I don't really myself find the divergences between the appearances more than what one would expect, given a whole lot of different psychic experiences which are told independently.

H.M.: Well, I don't think this is the place at which we can go into details about particular stories. Though I've got a Greek New Testament here I just don't think that this occasion is amenable to this treatment. I think this is the sort of thing we might do afterwards.

J.R.: Could I just say that I don't think that the evidence suggests that these were purely private things? They were obviously shared experiences, and I think they had a real objectivity about them; and that's about all that one can really be *sure* of.

H.M.: I suppose you could say that these were either fabrications or hallucinations or that they were similar to psychic phenomena which have happened elsewhere; or what one might call *sui generis*, unique, not like anything else, and therefore not to be understood in terms of anything else.

Of course if it's the last possibility, then we can't usefully talk about them very much. (I do feel this about them if they were unique: you either accept them or you don't accept them, and there you are.) I believe myself that we can rule out (others may not) that they're fabrications. I think that this is totally out of keeping with what people were like in the primitive church. We therefore seem to be left with the thought that they're either hallucinations or similar to other psychic phenomena, or unique. I myself can't see why most people won't take seriously the fact that they are similar in form, though not in meaning, to other psychic phenomena of people appearing shortly after they are dead. What do you make for instance of the fact that Jesus doesn't appear to anyone but his friends? This seems to me to be a remarkable fact. According to the evidence of the New Testament, he only appears to his friends. Do you see any significance in that.

J.R.: Yes, I think that this is true of a lot of psychic phenomena. There are a great many subjective conditions and unless there is some kind of relationship already established people just don't see these things. I think that the only thing I want to say about this is that people hesitate to say that they are just psychic phenomena because most psychic phenomena are so utterly futile and trivial. It is only in so far as they point beyond to a spiritual reality which seems to me to be on a very different plane that I personally am interested in psychic phenomena. Nevertheless they are the kind of thing that you do get cropping up in history and in experience as a result of a powerful personality. His effect upon those who have known him is that they go on having such experiences, although for a limited time.

H.M.: I was only suggesting a possible similarity in the mode of the appearances, not in the meaning of the appearances. The meaning seems to be utterly different because it's not a sort of trivial banality. There are commands from the risen Christ to go and do something usually, and hardly any of the appearances are evidential, at least in the way that they are written down. Well, the appearances form only one side of the evidence, do they not? There is also the story of the empty tomb, which you think St. Paul knew although he doesn't in fact seem to me to mention it explicitly. Now traditionally the empty tomb has, I suppose, been more important to most people than the appearances because they have felt that here is a bit of rock-like evidence—literally, because the stone was removed: that's something you cannot get by. Well, let's talk about that. The empty tomb appears in all four Gospels. We've got to consider how the story arose, whether it began because it actually happened, and if it didn't arise because it actually happened how anybody could have made it up in the form in which it now appears. Here is my difficulty about it. Personally, I cannot believe that an empty tomb is the foundation of the Christian faith: I think the living Christ is the foundation of the Christian faith, not something empty. But let's consider the empty tomb. I suppose there are other possible explanations. Would you like to say anything about them and what you think about them? I mean, you might say that Jesus was not dead and that somehow he removed that stone—it *has* been said —or that they went to the wrong tomb and that was why Mary Magdalene thought the gardener was really the gardener, or that the Jews stole it, or the disciples stole it, or that this was the kind of myth in which this belief in the living Jesus was bound to be expressed, using myth in a sense of a story, a concrete reality. If you are going to try to 'body it out' in a story then you would have to put it in these terms. Would you like to say anything about these alternative explanations?

J.R.: Well, you have given me a great many! I think a lot can, quite honestly, be dismissed because the 'credibility gap' is just too great—such as the idea that they invented the story as a deliberate fabrication, or that they were deceived, or that they were so stupid to go to the wrong tomb and never bother to check up, or that Jesus never died (in that case you've got to say what did happen to him afterwards). So many of these things seem to me to involve such a credibility gap that the Christian faith could never have got going at all, let alone be sustained against the obvious objections. But there are other explanations which I think one has got to take seriously. One of the most common today—and it was in fact given a good airing in the excerpt in *The Observer* on Easter Day from a new book by Colin Cross *Who was Jesus?*—runs something as follows. This is a

story made up in order to 'body forth' the faith the early
Christians believed because this is how a Jew *must* have
understood resurrection. So an account of it is invented later
in order to add verisimilitude. Now I think there are a lot
of questions to ask about this. First of all, when did the
story arise? There is a great deal of talk as though this is
late in the tradition; Bultmann and others argue like this.
I'm not at all convinced that you can dispose of it as easily
as that. As I said earlier, I think that St. Paul probably did
assume it in the words which he skirts over very lightly in
1 Corinthians 15:4 that 'he was buried ... and the third day
he rose again.' Now in all the accounts there's a great deal
of stress on the burial, in fact it's one of the best-attested
facts about Jesus. It's not only in the early preaching of
Acts and in St. Paul but also in all the Gospels, and there
are some very circumstantial accounts of it. It seems to me
quite absurd to say that it was just as likely that he was
thrown into a lime-pit. What does seem to me to be significant is that, given the fact that Paul had some sort of tradition about the tomb, why did he apparently make nothing
of it? In the second half of 1 Corinthians 15 there is a
long discussion of the relation between what he calls the
'natural body' and the 'spiritual body' in connection with
believers. Yet he never draws out any parallel with Christ
himself. This hardly reflects a strong motivation in the early
Church to create or elaborate the story. In fact when you get
it in the Gospels—and you get it in St. Mark, which is after
all the earliest Gospel tradition—it seems to be much more
something that the evangelists had on their hands which
they still found it difficult to make much of. The remarkable thing about the empty tomb is that, so far from prov-
ing the resurrection, it merely left those who found it in
dismay and disorder. And if the early Christians invented
this story it seems to me that they could have invented it
in a much more cogent form. First of all they based it on
the evidence of women, which in Jewish law didn't carry
any weight at all, and they didn't implicate the disciples. In
St. Mark the women didn't even tell them, in St. Luke they
told them and the disciples didn't believe it, in St. Matthew
they told them but the message was not 'Go and look at the
tomb' but 'Go to Galilee'. And in fact it isn't used as
evidence of the resurrection. It's only later in the light of the

appearances that people begin, as it were, to interpret this apparently meaningless and bewildering occurrence in terms of resurrection.

H.M.: Yes, I don't think I have anything really to add. I'm always puzzled by 'the third day' because it really is the most obscure text of Hosea that seems to be alluded to, and the idea that this text could ever give rise to a belief that something happened on the third day seems to me to be extraordinary: and I am puzzled how 'the third day' actually came in unless something actually did happen on the third day.

J.R.: Well, I agree, particularly as in Mark the so-called pre-dictions of the resurrection are 'after three days' which is in fact not what happened; and then you get in Matthew and Luke this altered to 'the third day' in the light of the event. It seems to me the event which in fact controlled things and not any predictions or prophecies.

H.M.: What I think we ought to go on to ask is, can we give any kind of rationale of the empty tomb? Is this event, if it is an event, wholly beyond our comprehension? When we die our bodies won't disappear. At least if they did the undertakers would be out of business, but quite apart from that we know that they won't disappear. Now what did it mean? What, if we may ask the question, was the point of the empty tomb other than an evidential point of resurrection? And yet when we look at the Gospels we see it isn't used evidentially.

J.R.: I would take the tradition of the empty tomb very seriously. In other words, I don't think they just invented it. And they had some embarrassment to know what to do with it. On the other hand, I don't think that this necessarily means one must give a supernaturalist explanation of it. I mean, it may have been empty for all sorts of reasons. The first thing the women think of is that there has been some dirty work: 'Where have you taken him and what have you done with him?' And it seems to me that there is an element of uncertainty and doubt which hangs over all this which is never cleared up. I don't think we can ever be sure that in fact it wasn't due to grave robbers or all kinds of things that might have happened. I think one can rule out *some* things, because as I say the credibility gap is too great. But it seems to me that we shall never know for certain. I think we must be prepared to be agnostic about this. To me nothing ultimately really hangs on this, and if in fact the bones of Jesus do lie around somewhere in Palestine, well, this honestly doesn't affect my belief in the spiritual reality of the resurrection; and, as you say, the idea that there couldn't have been resurrection unless Jesus's whole body somehow evaporated certainly doesn't correlate with any hope that the New Testament holds out for us and for our incorporation into Christ's resurrection. And therefore I would say that, so far as this being absolutely necessary for belief in the resurrection, in some ways it's a real source of difficulty. I personally think it most probable that they did find the tomb empty, that they found this utterly bewildering, but that in the light of their subsequent conviction of the spiritual reality they then interpreted this otherwise unsolved mystery as a sign that God indeed had been at work. But exactly what happened we shall never know and I don't think it really matters.

H.M.: And so really we come back almost to where we started, that what matters is the risen Christ, what mattered to them and what matters to us; and here we see God at work, we see God vindicating Jesus's death. We've been talking about the resurrection and we can't see the resurrection without looking at what happened when Jesus died— I'm sure you will agree there—and we see it as God's 'Yes' really to Jesus Christ and what he did and why he died.

J.R.: Yes, it seems to me that the heart of the thing is that what is embodied in Christ is something over which death has no power. What happened to the old body is as irrelevant as the chrysalis that's left behind. It's the butterfly that I'm interested in. And this seems to me to be a spiritual reality which is irrepressible and it is a power which is open to be shared now by all those who are prepared to expose themselves to it.

H.M.: Well, I think that we must leave it there. I seem to remember that after Paul's speech on the resurrection on Mars Hill, they said, 'We will hear you further on this,' and so let's break off the formal discussion at this point ...

CHAPTER THREE

HOW CAN MODERN MAN PRAY?

by Archbishop ANTHONY BLOOM,
Metropolitan of Sourozh

'How can modern man pray?' One can put the inflection in many ways. It may be a question, or it may be an exclamation—how indeed can man pray in the face of what is going on, while he is accusing God of everything that is wrong in the world? When we ask ourselves in this exclamatory way where our problems lie, then, perhaps we can face them and see whether we can answer this question, however partially.

First of all, may I say that modern man *does* pray? I have been reading lately a passage from a little pamphlet on prayer dialogue written in the U.S.A. by Cynthia and Theodore Wedell who have specialised in teaching dialogue prayer. It starts with a remark which I have never made myself and a thought which I had never come across. It says, 'Man does pray all the time, the only thing is that he doesn't realise either that he is praying or whom he is praying to.' And then they go on to point out against a background of Romans 8, that whenever with all our being, with all our passion, with all our desire we strive for something, we cry in prayer, 'Give, grant, let it happen'; but this prayer is very often directed simultaneously in two opposite directions. On the one hand we turn to God with a twofold prayer. 'If it is at all possible, O Lord, let it happen.' On the other hand, as a security, when we are pious enough but not frank enough or straight enough we add, 'And thy will be done.' This means: 'I have not much hope to defeat your will, so let it be done, let me be on the safe side anyhow.' But at the same time, somewhere deep in us there is another prayer going on. It's not addressed to the Lord God in terms of security or pressurising. It's on the other side. Very often while we say, 'O God, let it happen,' we say to the adversary, 'Satan, make it happen, help me. All my greed is at stake, all my lust is

at stake, all my fear and feeling is at stake. Make it happen';
and then we turn back to God and say, 'If we can find a
way of doing so, let it happen; yet thy will be done.' I think
it's very important to realise how continually we pray. Whenever with all the desire of our being we want and beg and
long for something, then it is a prayer. It may be the Holy
Spirit in unfathomable groanings is trying to pierce through
to express and articulate within us what God really wants
for us, but it may also be the whisperings of the powers of
darkness who say, 'Try, try again to break the resistances
of God. I will help.'

I remember a man who once came to our midnight service
—Easter night it was. I believe he was a tramp; a rather
doubtful character, not because he was a tramp but because
he was such. He stood there in Church as the service began
and I came out and greeted the people: 'Christ is risen.'
I put quite a lot of conviction in it because I believe he is
risen and I rejoice in it. And the people responded by saying, 'He is risen indeed.' So he told me that when I came
out and shouted, he said to himself, 'He is paid for that.'
And when he heard the response, he said to himself, 'That's
the old people probably.' Then he looked around and saw
that quite a lot of young people were shouting passionately
their faith that Christ is risen indeed, and then he said that
the thought came to him, 'My goodness, if that's true and
I let myself go, I will have to change my life.' So he tried
not to and then he heard himself howl, 'Christ is risen
indeed,' and he felt he was lost. He said to me, 'Then I
turned to the Devil and said, 'Look, you have been my help
throughout my life. Come to my rescue now.' And he added,
'The dirty brat didn't come.' Now that is exactly what I
mean about this complex state of prayer in which we are.
On the one hand we might be overwhelmed by our conviction of God's presence, of other people's witness, of something within us stirring deeply; and at the same time we
feel how dangerous all that would be if it were true. If you
want chapter and verse look up Isaiah, look up St. Paul, who
both say that it is a dreadful thing to fall into the hands of
the living God. It's exactly what that man said. 'The dirty
brat didn't come to my rescue.' He felt he was caught, his
double prayer was now judgment, he had to face the truth
of life or the truth of death. He had to face his own experi-

ence of something and he could not reject it without the help of the Devil, and the Devil couldn't help.

Now if it is true that there are two spirits at war, then prayer begins much earlier than we realise. It begins at the root of our being when with all our energies and passions we long and wish and claim and cry for something to happen or to be given. That explains perhaps why there are circumstances in which we pray spontaneously and easily when a great joy comes upon us, when a bereavement hits at us, when what has happened is so overwhelming that we can't give a thought to what others will think of us, or when we can't give a thought to what we will think of ourselves later when we become stale and half dead. Then prayer bursts out of us. It may be a word of prayer, a cry, a shout, it may be a more elaborate form of prayer, but it is prayer. Then it is easy because for one moment by the pain or by the joy we have been brought back inside ourselves, and inside ourselves we have forgotten the onlooker because it matters too much.

Now if that is true then something very important is also true, that it is impossible for us to pray very often because we are very seldom within ourselves. Most of the time we are beside ourselves. We don't act from within, we don't act from the depths, we don't act really by our choice; most of the time we don't act, we react. We act because something has happened and we respond to it. This is not the sovereign freedom of a free act, it is conditioned. It is nothing to do with us except that we passively receive an impact and in a half-active way respond to it. We must learn to have such inwardness as to be able to act freely of our own choice to wield it.

I have said a minute ago that we are most of the time beside ourselves. What does that mean? In the eary 1930s a French scientist working in the U.S.A. wrote a book called *Man the Unknown*. The name of the scientist is Alexis Carell (he also wrote later a book on prayer). He said somewhere that we are under a delusion most of the time that we are self-contained, that our personality is limited, as it were, to where our skin covers our body. It is not true, he said. Don't you realise, he said, that the whole digestive system of a greedy person, instead of being located within his body, is spread throughout the world? His tentacles cling to all the edibles of the world. Don't you realise that all the senses of a curious person are like tentacles clinging to everything that may be an object of curiosity, so that in the end we can describe a man very much like an octopus? He is a cavity in an expectant emptiness related to the outer world by tentacles that hold on solidly to what they have caught. Now there are two things that have happened in the process. The moment you catch something with your tentacles you imagine that you have laid hold of it. In reality you haven't, because it is you who are caught, not the thing that you have taken. Suppose I take this watch and clench my fist on it. What happens? I have got the security of a watch, but I have lost the use of my hand and arm and the use of my shoulder. I can do nothing else but hold the watch with quite a lot of bone and muscle that could be used for much more than that. There is a story in the old Persian legends about a young man who goes out for a journey. He comes back stripped to the bone. 'But couldn't you defend yourself? What did you do about the robbers?' 'Well,' he said in indignation, 'I had a dagger in one hand and a pistol in the other.' That sounds like a joke but isn't it exactly what we do in life? We cling to things, we hold them, and if we have closed our heart solidly on one unique thing, it's no use for anything else. If we close our brain in the same way on a few things it is no use any more, not to speak of our hands in all forms of activity. When you have made the object of your pursuit, say, status values, what is left of you? There is no space for anything else.

And so there is a problem before we can stand before God. There must be something apart from this inward empti-ness of the octopus to put before God. If there is nothing but the emptiness what is going to stand before God? What is going to pray to God? What is going to speak to God? And so there is a real problem to become free that begins there; not to become detached, simply to be free, not to be like Gulliver lying on the ground and tied by each of his hairs to blades of grass each of which is so frail that we could tear it with two fingers, but which in their together-ness keep him a prisoner of the world of little men. That is our first problem if we want to stand before God who is all freedom and who claims a relationship of freedom: to free ourselves, not to be slaves, so then we can begin to think about praying. And to do that we must start by little things, not by the enormous great things which we always undertake because it is safe to undertake great things; we are sure we won't achieve them and it will give us evidence that the best thing is to do nothing. We are quite prepared to command all the mountains of the world to cast themselves into the seas. As to doing something small enough and real enough we aren't prepared to do it.

Well, let us start then with the simplest and humblest thing in the world. As St. John Chrysostom puts it, 'Give to God what you don't need at all.' It will first of all not rob you of much, and secondly, it will give you no chance to be proud. If you want an example taken from life, my mother worked for a literary agent who had a mother-in-law who was a Belgian lady. At the age of ninety-seven she was bed-ridden, but read without glasses and did her business by correspondence. She was a very orderly lady and when she died everything was in order. In one corner of the room there was a nice cardboard box tied with a string and label inscribed 'little pieces of string that can no longer be put to any use'. Now haven't we got, all of us, somewhere, little bits of string that can't be put to any use? And don't we cling to them with one of the many tentacles because an octopus is nothing compared with us?—we are centipedes, centi-tentacled creatures. Well, let go of these, and you will see that you have got one tentacle which is free, which you can bring back to live in peace. If you do that gradually you will discover that you have started your journey *inwards*, that you are beginning to discover that you have got something inside you. Mind you, you won't enjoy it at once because what happens usually in this descent into hell or in this journey inwards is that when we have begun to let go of a few things we feel remarkably free, rather like someone who has cast some ballast off. It's lighter, it's more peaceful, one has a certain number of hands. Then the peace and the silence and the quietness of it begin to be worrying because we are not used to being quiet or silent or peaceful. And then after a while when we have stayed with our own selves long enough we begin to feel bored! This is a remarkable moment because it could teach us a lesson which is infinitely precious, if we could only realise how bored we are when we are faced with ourselves. Wouldn't it explain to us why we are so bored when we are left with ourselves alone? That would be a good, useful lesson, it would not be in vain, we could even make allowances for God when he doesn't come when he is summoned by us. We might perhaps say he has known us so long and been so bored. It's not quite a joke because what we usually do is that we discover in a certain moment of idleness that we could spare five minutes for God. Then we turn to him and make, according to the height of our churchmanship, a sign of the cross, a genuflection or nothing at all, and we look round with an air of surprise. 'What? isn't God there yet?' That's not the way of learning to pray, he will never be there for us in the void, he must meet someone who has some sort of reality or consistency. That can be done only if we go inward beyond the boredom. And beyond the boredom do you know what you will find? You will find fear, because the moment you go beyond your boredom you discover within yourself a looming abyss, an emptiness that is dark, still unknown, undiscovered; and you will have to go into that abyss. This abyss has got, if I may put it this way, two aspects. On the one hand it is simply the looming emptiness of that naught out of which God's creative Word has called us and above which he keeps us alive. In that sense, if there is nothing but this naught and this emptiness, we are doomed; we will fall into this bottomless pit and never reach the end of it and be lost. You may remember in *The Descent into Hell* by Charles Williams the way in which in the end Wentworth falls into the naught, eternally falling, never reaching its depths. But if we go into this depth with courage and faith, with the certainty that the unseen is there and that the invisible is alive, we will discover that this inward emptiness of ours is far too great, far too big for us, because, as the Archbishop of Canterbury once put it, 'it is a God-shaped emptiness.' It is as vast as the divine presence, it has the shape of God, it cannot be filled with anything but God himself. And if going into that depth we begin to cry God-words, if we say, 'Come, come because you alone can fill this darkness. You alone can be the presence in this total absence and dereliction,' then we will learn something about prayer.

There is another thing that seems to prevent modern man from praying. It is his inability to cope with time. There is no time. But there is plenty of it. I remember a Jehovah's Witness who came to see me, and after a long talk I hoped I could get loose and said, 'Well, you're so kind, I don't want to waste any more of your time,' and the girl said to me, 'Don't worry, sir, I have plenty of time. It isn't mine it's God's,' which filled me with real anguish! Well, the fact is we don't know how to live within the present moment, that is the problem. I'm not going to speak to you at all about the way you can use time which we waste otherwise. If it was just a question of time everyone would have twenty minutes to pray in his bath, so many minutes while he is doing nothing and so forth. No, there is another problem of time—a subjective sense of time because we are in a hurry, not because three minutes will go by in less than three minutes but because I am tense inside and because there are minutes that jump and there are others that crawl—that is the problem. Now the first thing we must realise about time is that time does not run away from us, time comes our way. You don't need to run away from this sermon. In a few minutes my time will be over and you will be free and yet you have done nothing, you have been sitting with greater or lesser patience. Time comes our way like a river that brings at every moment the next moment into our hands. So if instead of running after the time that is coming towards us we just stand where we are and live within the present moment, we will have an infinite succession of rich, present moments instead of having a sequence of moments that are already in the past, which we have not filled with any content, as well as moments which are still in the future which are still yet out of reach.

The second important matter is that we must know how to stop time. I have learnt something about it at the very blessed moment when I was arrested in the Underground during the German Occupation. At that moment I discovered something extremely interesting. The past which was my real past was a thing I would deny and therefore it wasn't there any more. The past I would expound lavishly is that past that would never have been, so it wasn't there anyhow. So there was no past. I began really here. As to the future I discovered that there is a future only if you can foresee a split second beforehand what may happen; but when you can foresee nothing and imagine nothing, when expectation is just a blank, then there is no future. If you add to this the fact that being arrested is being a moment when all your energies are being concentrated on getting away, then you discover that the present moment acquires a density, an intensity that is simply marvellous. This is a discovery of the present, that is something we must all try to discover. You can discover that even without the privilege of being arrested by the Gestapo. It is not something that you can manufacture. But you can learn to stop time. How? Very simply, at the moment when you have nothing to do, when you are safe, you close your door and you say, 'I drop out of time into God's presence.' This is the point where time in eternity meets the present moment, and for five minutes I will not allow myself anything except just being within myself in God's presence whatever happens. 'Whatever happens' means that the telephone may ring, the front doorbell may ring and so forth. Well, suppose, you are not there! Actually that is true because you are in heaven so you don't even need to lie if you put a note on your door, 'I am not there.' If you have more courage you could do what my father did. He had in a permanent place a note on his door, 'Don't knock, I am there, but I shan't open.' Well, once you are there in the present moment you sit down and you make yourself relax, you let all the tensions go. You sit and you let your hands, your shoulders and your whole body come to a state of peace; and then you recollect the presence of God in a sort of alert attitude which is no longer tension. The image I could give you is taken from one of our Russian divines who said, 'One must be and live in life like a violin string rightly tuned, neither slack nor overtense so that the moment you touch it it can give clearly, neatly, the right note.' That is the whole problem. Once you have learnt that, you stay in that state for a few minutes until you have learned to be in God's presence and absent from the whole world as long as you need, as long as you choose. And you will discover that 'the round world will not be shaken by its foundations' because you have dropped out of it. Nothing will happen. It's even rather distressing.

Once you have learnt that, try the next step. Try to stop time during the moments when it presses on you, when you are doing something, when you must do something. Say 'maliciously', 'I won't, I shall stop whatever I need to do, I'm not going to do it.' Exactly what you do when you want to go to the cinema, you stop and you learn 'maliciously' to be in God's presence, 'maliciously' in the sense that you are not doing anything useful for the salvation and good of the whole world. And you will discover that one can quite soon rapidly, almost instantaneously drop into that inwardness, that stability, that silence, that collectedness which is the present moment. And when you will have discovered the way inward and the way to this stability, you will discover that at any moment you can be in that state whatever you do and whatever is done to you.

If you try to take into account the few things I have said you will discover that modern man can pray. There is an additional reason for this. We are modern because every generation before us said also that they were modern and that they were quite new and unheard of. Indeed, each of us feels that. But the marvellous thing about God is that he is contemporary with every modern generation. He is never outdated. He never waxes old. He is not like the clergy who may be outmoded. He is new, fresh and contemporary with us at every century and every day of our life. So assume that God is your contemporary, that he understands a great deal more about the contemporary situation of the world than you do and certainly knows you a great deal more than you know yourself, when you are in the octopus state. Stand in the present moment within yourself, with all your life, all your problems, all your energies collected and facing the totality of life of which God is part, and which God pervades completely because he is involved, committed and active in everything. One of the reasons why we find it so difficult to meet him is that he is committed to the hilt but we are not. We are prepared to be involved in life up to a point, like the French writer Rabelais, 'I am prepared to stand for my convictions up to death exclusively.' God is prepared to stand for his convictions up to death inclusively and he has given evidence of it. He has become man, he has died; we have never come near any sort of involvement of that kind.

So when you feel frightfully involved, ask yourself where is God's involvement, and go further than yourself to the place where he is, at the breaking point of every tragic situation. Put yourself there, recollect totally the present moment face to face with life and God and yourself, and you will see that prayer will spring out of you whether you want it or not; and you will discover that man can pray the moment he becomes man and ceases to be an octopus.

CHAPTER FOUR

CHASTITY—OR FREE LOVE?

by Dr. KENNETH SODDY,
Consultant Child Psychiatrist,
University College Hospital, London

In the 7th chapter of the first Epistle to the Corinthians, St. Paul wrote (according to the New English Bible translation):

> 'It is a good thing for a man to have nothing to do with women; but because there is so much immorality, let each man have his own wife and each woman her own husband.'

It would be difficult to find anywhere a more belittling view of Christian marriage; though in quoting him out of context I may be doing the writer as much injustice as he did to his subject. Of course, St. Paul was expecting the second coming of Christ at any moment, and in his anxiety to do as much as possible in a limited time he had a campaigner's impatience with camp followers, and no sense of commitment to posterity. Moreover, as the lesson (1 Cor. 6:12-20) has shown, he did have other thoughts on the subject.

But this and other passages of a similar order in the New Testament are often quoted and acted upon out of context. Actually Paul went no further here than to say that while celibacy was best, marriage was better than burning with 'vain desire'.

It was some of the Church Fathers who elaborated the 'badness' of the body into what Christopher Driver referred to in a recent article in the *Guardian* as a 'literature of self-disgust', developed by Augustine and, much later, by Aquinas and 'reaffirmed down the centuries within a celibate subculture which was sheltered alike from ordinary family experience and from the rise of modern science, both biological and psychological'. Driver pointed out that Roman Catholics, 'in particular, are invited to accept more or less uncritically a sexual code handed down from the Fathers of the Church but are not trained to assess these extraordinary men as victims—like the rest of us—of a particular historical environment'.

It is the historical environment that I mainly want to consider but, first, some definitions of *chastity* and *free love*. The first meaning given to chastity in the eight-volume *Oxford English Dictionary* is 'purity from unlawful sexual intercourse'. The *Concise Oxford Dictionary*, although giving chastity as continence; 'virginity, celibacy; simplicity of style or taste', defines the adjective chaste as 'abstaining from unlawful or immoral (also from all) sexual intercourse, pure, virgin . . .'. The legal side is foremost, too, in the definition of free love, which is simply 'sexual relations irrespective of marriage'.

If chastity means abstention from, and free love means entering into sex relations outside of marriage, our title offers little scope for law-abiding people to discuss. The last thing I want to do is to challenge or belittle the institution of marriage. Every human society, as far as I know, orders and controls the sexual activities of its members; and our society has for centuries settled for a lifelong monogamous union strictly supported by morality and law.

Let us consider human relationships rather than legal institutions. First, is sexual intercourse primarily a function of marriage or an act of love? We are told that the idea of marriage for love is of comparatively recent origin in Europe and is by no means the rule everywhere there, even today. The concept of romantic love itself dates merely from the Middle Ages, and in those days of small communities and poor communications, romantic love can have had very little to do with sexual intercourse. Even in highly urbanised and socially mobile Britain, only during the current century has any weight of responsible opinion developed that sexual intercourse is more importantly a function of love than of marriage.

Historically, Christian notions of marriage and sexual behaviour were derived from a 1st-century Israel—fighting for cultural survival—but reflected the *mores* of a nomadic desert people of the time of Moses. In this miniscule nomadic society everyone knew everyone else, everybody and everything had to be highly mobile; conditions of life were harsh

and unforgiving; the slightest departure from the protection of the tribal society—either geographically or in
behaviour—meant certain death. The family head had to be
the absolute master in his own household, the security of
which required complete obedience. At the same time,
because of his vulnerability and brief expectation of life, his
authority needed the support of the conservative rigidity of
the female members of the household.

Could there be a historical environment more different
from our own as a basis on which to construct our notions
of natural law, or the will of God, or what you will? Inter-
estingly, in the incident of the woman taken in adultery,
Jesus reacted with no more than a gentle reminder of the
importance of conformity in a society which tolerated no
non-conformity.

This 'celibate sub-culture', as Driver termed the leader-
ship of Western Christendom, in spite of much rationalisa-
tion, seems never to have got away from the feeling that
sexual intercourse is essentially bad—only permissible when
procreation is the aim, subject only to the concession that
exploitation of the euphemistically termed 'safe period' is
not forbidden. Jerome's view that man degrades woman by
love-making (I quote): 'If we abstain from coitus we honour
our wives; if we do not abstain—well, what is the opposite
of honour but insult?', was, to the surprise of many, echoed
in the worry expressed in the recent encyclical lest widespread use of the 'pill' would result in abuse of woman for
man's sensual pleasure.

Although the 'celibate sub-culture' lost its influence in
many parts of Christendom after the Reformation, much of
its sexual anxiety has persisted; though an exception is to
be found in our Elizabethan marriage service—'with my
body I thee worship'. It seems to me that there has been a
persistent wish that people would obey 'God's law'—as
promulgated by the Fathers of the Church! Though whether
this be God's law or more realistically the code of nomadic,
desert tribes modified through the centuries in Mediterranean
societies with extended and hierarchical families is an un-
settled question of some importance.

But some of the reasons why the English have never been
able to accept these near-Eastern and Mediterranean models
have been indicated by Peter Laslett in his fascinating study,

The World We Have Lost. Laslett has produced evidence
that for at least 400 years the English family has had a so-
called 'nuclear' structure—parents and small children living
together during the latter's dependency in more or less independent, two-generation, groups. A large sample of parish
registers of the 17th and 18th centuries revealed that in no
community did the number of households that included more
than two generations reach ten per cent of the whole. Few
even approached that percentage, and it was evidently a
social imperative that the young leave home, at latest, by
the time of marriage.

Such a way of life would quickly result in social breakdown—perhaps even moral chaos—unless the moral sanctions of these young people came from within themselves
rather than from external authority. This imperative for the
individual to assume responsibility for himself was much
increased by the short expectation of life. Laslett found that
35.5 per cent of the children living in Clayworth in May
1688 had lost at least one parent while still dependent. Broken
homes abounded. But nothing like moral chaos has ever been
reported.

There are, of course, other kinds of moral sanction; for
example, what of the neighbours, the 'what will other people
say?' kind of concern. But this kind of sanction, which has
been developed to a terrifying degree in Soviet types of social
organisation, is generally incompatible with so-called
'nuclear' families. Without rigid political machinery, such
sanctions can be effective only in small, self-contained communities that do not change much, and at times and places
when and where communications and movement are not
easy. Here Laslett again has challenged conventional thinking by finding evidence of great social mobility in 17th-
century England. For example, sixty-one per cent of the
people living in Clayworth, Nottinghamshire, in 1688 had
not been there twelve years earlier, and at Cogenhoe, North-
ants, fifty per cent of those living there in 1628 had not been
there ten years earlier. Allowing for normal mortality this
means that a third of the population of Clayworth in 1676
died within twelve years and a third moved somewhere else.

If, as appears to have been the case, it was generally true
of pre-industrial England that late teenagers were separated
from their parents, and that the volume of internal migration

was very considerable, how much more potent were these factors to become after the industrial revolution, which was accompanied by a five-fold rise in population and huge areas of new conurbation into and out of which the population poured? The patriarch—if he ever existed—could not accompany his offspring into the new life, a circumstance which greatly increased the importance of the young men and women assuming responsibility for their own moral conduct, at the latest, by the end of the teenage period. This ultimate necessity for moral sanctions to be internal has resulted in the very obvious weakness of patriarchal authority in our family life and in our society generally. Remote *ex cathedra* pronouncements about God's law fall on ears that are hard of hearing in a society in which the culture has placed moral responsibility on the individual. Unless the moral principle is itself in the hearts and minds of individuals, invocation of obedience to authority can be no more than one factor influencing decisions—unnecessary in the case of responsible people, and unlikely to influence those, less responsibly minded, who pay attention only to sanctions that hurt.

Ironically, in England it has been only since Hardwicke's Marriage Act of 1753 that a religious ceremony has generally been regarded as an essential prelude to sexual intercourse. An older, more prevalent, usage was the espousal or contract publicly entered into before witnesses and marked by the kissing of the woman by the man and the presentation of gifts which constituted a binding marriage, provided only that the couple then proceeded to sexual intercourse. This form of marriage contract was expressly forbidden by the Roman Catholic Church after the Council of Trent in 1564, after which cohabitation by an affianced couple, whatever their intentions, was a grave sin. But in Protestant England it was the understanding arrived at between the couple, or, in other words, the quality of the relationship between them, that gave them the moral right to sexual intimacy.

However, it would be idle to deny that by the middle of the 19th century the great majority in this country would have regarded sexual intercourse before or outside religious marriage as morally wrong. Laslett comments: 'It would be a nice study in social development and local variation to discover how it was that the rule of the Catholic Church established itself as the moral imperative of the Protestant Christian ...'

According to Laslett, parish records show that pre-nuptial pregnancy rates could be substantial. Among 976 baptisms of the first child (normally three weeks after birth) recorded at Colyton in Devon between 1538 and 1799, 46.2 per cent took place within eight months of the parents' marriage, and 61.3 per cent within nine months. There can be no doubt about the pre-nuptial sexual activity in that village, especially when one adds on the number of couples who must have arranged the baptism elsewhere, and all the embryos and babies that for one reason or another did not survive. Even if the general level were only, say, a quarter of the Colyton figures, it would not be possible to sustain the view that premarital intercourse was taboo in those days. The Victorians seem to have been sterner about it, and one wonders why. It can hardly have been a religious reason, because during the Puritan ascendancy the importance attached to the Sacraments declined, and, indeed, many 17th- and 18th-century Nonconformists thought the marriage service irrelevant.

I think that it was the law—secular law—in other words the compulsory registration of marriage, birth and death, that was mainly responsible for the change in attitude. Perhaps the most important factor has been the requirement that one's birth certificate be produced on occasion. Until quite lately the birth certificate has been potentially a terrible punitive instrument—to punish the wrong person. But though religious leaders may have taken advantage of these powerful sanctions, it has not been religion, but regulation —not Love but Law—that has impinged on the individual. And in our culture, as we have discussed, the sanctions of external authority are not the strongest ones.

On the other hand, it would be foolish to claim that present-day attitudes about extra-marital sexual intercourse are not creating serious problems, especially in the larger towns, and among young men and women in their late teens and early twenties. Obviously social mobility has increased enormously, and the restraints on sexual behaviour exerted in the past by what the neighbours might see and think, by convention and by chaperonage, are useless in a community where you do not know your neighbours and where you have no roots. The boy–girl relationships that sanctioned sexual intercourse in the 17th century had probably lasted several years, and, moreover, both parties knew what the marriage market was like and could make their decisions accordingly. Today in a large town how is a girl to know soon whether an affair is sufficiently established to warrant sexual intercourse—or should she wait for 'Mr. Right'?

Nowadays, also, greater social equality of the sexes and, most of all, effective and available contraception independent of the male, have completely altered the situation. We now need, as we have never before needed, more sanctions that are internal so that they are an essential part of our own value systems. We must face the fact that our community has lost its effective legal and social sanctions to control sexual behaviour, and religious sanctions have not been really effective here for more than 400 years. Moreover, the recent row in Roman Catholic circles over the 'pill' encyclical shows how very improbable it is that religious sanctions once discredited can be reinstated, even in a social climate in which authority is acceptable.

It is generally accepted that no human society allows man's instinctual drives to be expressed directly, without modification, direction and inner control. No man or woman can satisfy any urge or desire without first estimating the consequences, and considering moral and social acceptability, and so on. Even hunger, the strongest of all manifestations of instinctual drive, is civilised and domesticated. How has this come about, and does the process throw any light on how sex might be managed better? Ironically, it seems to me that most of us do, in fact, control our sex drives by much the same principles by which we have civilised our hunger, and would that some of our religious leaders would ponder this more!

Let us look, briefly, at how hunger drives become civilised. Between the ages of three and six months a baby begins to recognise objects, discriminate between different experiences and remember things; very shadowy at first, of course, but a beginning. At each feed, say four to five times a day, his hunger discomfort is replaced by a feeling of bodily bliss. This feeling apparently gains in strength until by nine months, if things go well, by responding pleasurably to the presence of his mother, whether he is hungry or not, the baby shows that he has associated his recurrent feeding experiences with his bodily feelings, and both with his mother. This baby is strongly motivated to communicate— not only to receive food but also to watch out for and respond to the other signals his mother makes, to give signals himself and share in her joyful response. As a result, both parties move swiftly to the point at which it is their relationship rather than the giving and taking of food that gives them both bliss. Our baby is by now already on the way to appreciate Omar Khayyam's view that a jug of wine, a loaf of bread— and thou—makes the wilderness into a paradise, and is better than having supper with the sultan. There is here a striking reminder of Jesus's quotation, 'Man cannot live on bread alone; he lives on every word that God utters'. (N.E.B.).

Once hunger has been subordinated to the mother–child relationship—not without squalls, of course—the child has reached first base in his long climb towards civilised moral values. He has already gone beyond the simple body pain–pleasure principle. The child is highly motivated to attend to and learn from the parent, and to communicate in his turn. As the child grows in realisation of what the parents value and what behaviour evokes pleasurable parental reactions, he is increasingly motivated to please. To cut a long story short, eventually the child's system includes other members of the family, his peers, teachers, community leaders, and also transcendental values and moral abstractions.

Some aspects of children's upbringing experiences have more specifically moral connotations. For example, during toilet training, children learn that what they do by their own efforts is bad (ah! ah! says the mother, dirty!), but what they do mother's way, hygienically into a pot, is very good. Two of the possible implications of this for morality are: (1) the direct expression of instinctual drives is 'bad', but their expression in obedience to the most powerful influence on one's life is 'good'; (2) it is the relationship that really counts—the (good) relationship enables the (bad) instinctual drive to be expressed in ways that are not only meritorious but also enhance the interpersonal relationship. But in this case, unlike the case of hunger, the resulting body pleasure is not actively sought, it is merely tolerated, as 'respectable', as it were.

But not all children manage these things well; unhappy or unsatisfied children may not be able to sustain a quality of relationship that enables them to control and direct the expression of their hunger. They may well go in for compulsive sweet-eating, or some other form of auto-erotic behaviour, or later in life, solitary drinking or compulsive solitary cigarette and pipe or 'pot' smoking, or other self-compensating acts. These are all activities in which the self is engaged alone, and they have in common a possibility that they may impair or in some cases even destroy the individual's relationships.

At this point we come back to consider sex. When puberty arouses sexual hunger in quite specific directions, individuals may be faced with the very personal problem of how to express instinctual drives in ways that are acceptable both to society and to their own internal moral agency. Happily brought-up children have learned that to subordinate their drives to their relationship with the loved person is the surest way to maximum pleasure and satisfaction. Those who were not so happy as children may well be precipitated by increasing physiological sexual tensions into release-seeking behaviour. They may resort to masturbation, thus resembling (in another context) the compulsive sweet-eater five or ten years earlier, or to casual sexual intercourse, and in these ways may experience whatever pleasure the body can give them shorn of relationship enhancement, and also whatever guilt may result from religious or moral training. In neither case does the behaviour enrich their interpersonal relationships; quite the contrary. Increasingly today—if popular reports are to be believed, and there are no statistics available—when experiencing physiological tensions, young people of both sexes go straight to sexual intercourse, without paying any attention to the interpersonal relationships involved. In the *International Times* of April 5-18, 1968 (this, as you all know, is the organ of the Tribes), under the motto 'an orgasm a day', a writer devoted several hundred words to how to make the sexual act more meaningful. 'Normally,' he wrote, 'you feel you are an individual, separate, alone.' When I first read this, my eyes almost popped out of my head. This is Sex without Relationship. And this also, it seems to me, is where society can get to if it persists in its attempt to govern sex by the rule of law, whether religious or secular, and if the law is discredited and its enforcement measures have broken down in the community —which I believe to be the case here. Where sex is governed by the relationship, a very different situation obtains. Where two people are mutually highly identified with each other, the interests and well-being of the other party are the first consideration. In this type of relationship both parties are likely to be activated towards each other by the highest principles they know and not by the lowest. Their mutual love brings out the best in both. Their relationship is unique and specific to themselves alone, and they can bring into it only those principles and precepts which are at the heart of their respective beings; including, maybe, the conviction that sexual pleasure is 'good' and God-given. I don't think I need labour this!

And may I remind you that in a culture in which authority is transmitted in a patriarchal line, in Church, State and Family, authoritative or *ex cathedra* pronouncements may well be effective and binding upon the vast majority of individuals. But in a culture, such as our own, where tradition has strongly enhanced the responsibility and independence of the individual, the moral tone of society is maintained by the moral orientation of individual citizens rather than by exhortations from on high. These latter may be worse than useless, for they may even provoke negative reactions.

And so we return to our title, Chastity or Free Love, which I have considered in the context of the interpersonal relationship involved, and illustrated by reference to two types of control and direction of instinctual drives during childhood. In the case of hunger there is an implicit understanding that hunger drives are an essential human attribute and their satisfaction is 'good', desirable and enjoyable; all that is necessary is that the child indulge and express hunger in ways that enhance the relationship involved. In the case of toilet training, it is explicit that the matter involved is 'bad'; it may be made tolerable provided the rules are faithfully followed but neither 'good' nor unashamedly enjoyable. Control of bladder and bowels is expected of children, and success does little specific to enhance interpersonal relationships; failure tends to destroy them.

It has been a tragedy of Christendom that the prevailing attitude attached to the control and direction of sexual appetites has derived more from the latter—the toilet-training situation—than from the former—the management of food appetites. St. Paul said, 'It is a good thing for a man to have nothing to do with women'—he did not actually say that sex is bad, but the implication is there, nevertheless. What he did say, in effect, was: if you must do it, then do it this way; only thus can you avoid badness. He said nothing about enjoyment. Such a negative attitude has provided little protection in the face of one of the very strongest of human forces and it has required all the panoply of Church and State to hold the situation in check, even in the case of the faithful and the more law-abiding citizens respectively. Now that the ineffectiveness of religious, legal and social sanctions has been exposed to the view of all (except those who will not see), in our promotion of morality we are thrown back upon basic human relationships and the power of love. I would say 'Thank God' and—dare I add—'about time too'.

In other words, it is my conviction that if your generation can attend to the basic relationship formation of its children, and to the fostering of love and mutual respect in the family, the sexual behaviour of your succeeding generation will take care of itself far more effectively than even you will manage to do yourselves. The probable fact that your children's principles of sexual behaviour will bear little resemblance to those of the generation preceding my own (which is unfortunately what we tend to judge your generation by) is, I hope, a good, rather than a bad thing.

CHAPTER FIVE

WHAT KIND OF LOVING?

by the Very Reverend TONY BRIDGE, Dean of Guildford

What kind of loving? It is a good question; but before looking at it, there is an even more basic one which should be asked: namely, why love at all? or, rather, why value love at all? That may sound an idiotic question to ask in our own society. On the whole, we all assume without question, or nearly without question, that love is a virtue, let alone a joy, enrichment, and even staple food of the human psyche. But other civilisations have assumed no such thing. Courage, stoic endurance, the search for wisdom, intellectual integrity, strength, detachment—these are the virtues normally worshipped by mankind and preached by his many religions. And love is a contradiction of many of them. It makes a man weak, not strong, anyway from the military point of view, and thus disarms courage as usually defined and admired. Again and again it overrides intellect; hence such tags as 'love is blind'. It arouses too deep a set of emotions to be compatible with the kind of wisdom sought by the world's philosophers, and it wrecks any attempt to achieve the kind of detachment from the changes and chances of this mortal life so prized by the votaries of Eastern religions; for love inevitably leads to commitment and involvement, not detachment. So why do we assume that it is a virtue? Largely because, for several thousand years, it has been preached and believed to be such by both the Jewish and the Christian religions; but also and latterly because psychologists, too, have emphasised the enormous importance and value of love, both to personal fulfilment— even personal sanity—and to social stability and development. 'When Israel was a child, then I loved him,' cried Yahweh of the Jews to his people. 'I drew them with cords of a man, with bands of love.' 'God is love,' Christians have insisted ever since—and still insist. 'I don't know about God being love,' psychologists implicitly and sometimes even explicitly say, 'but certainly love is God, if by God you mean the ultimate need of men.' But apart from one great affirmation by the Buddha—one lyrically splendid passage—no one else agrees. That is worth remembering, if only as a warning to us to recall that our unquestioned assumption has very deep roots in Judaic–Christian belief, and to remember too that plants have a habit of dying when cut off from their roots, however skilful their psychological gardeners may be.

But now—what kind of loving? I speak as a man celebrating today his thirty-third wedding anniversary. There are two primary forms: parental and sexual, both quite plainly evolved over the millennia as aids to specific survival—and both, of course, good. I'm tempted to shout that loudly. For so many churchmen have given the impression to the world of being the most repressive kind of parents and the most bigoted opponents of sexual love and sexual pleasure that, even now, it is still important to do everything possible, even at the risk of sounding rather drearily with-it, to say how much in favour one is, as a Christian, of true parental love and true sexual love and pleasure. In fact, I must say that there seems to me to be no sexual pleasure debarred to a Christian so long as it is part of a real and true love. Which makes it possible, I hope, for me to say also that some parental 'love' and some sexual 'love' (the word love in quotes in both cases) can be lethal and extremely destructive: indeed, can be not love at all. For instance, parental 'love' which becomes so possessive that it feeds the ego of the parent while extinguishing the freedom of the child to be a separate and fulfilled person is not true love at all. Similarly, the sexual 'love' which at its worst treats the so-called beloved as a Kleenex handkerchief to be used once or twice at the most in order to cater for a physical need and then to be discarded is not love either. In other words, a measure of self-giving to the beloved as opposed to a total self-pandering at the expense of another person is the first requisite of love. Normally, much self-giving is present in both parental love, from which we first learn what love is, and in sexual love through which we learn even more about the death of self in love of another. But both have their origin in evolution which has produced them for a specific pur-

pose: the better survival of the species. And when the procreation of children and their infant care and protection have
been accomplished, both tend to lose their force and their
urgency. You could say that the emotions of parental love
and sexual love, especially the latter, are transitory—unless,
of course, they lead to something deeper and more lasting.

What they should, can, and often do lead to is more than
an emotion, though it is closely associated with the emotions
of tenderness, warmth, and the desire to cherish. It is a
state of mind and heart characterised even more than sexual
love by self-giving; but it is even more than an attitude of
mind and heart. It is a living realisation that one is no longer
one thing and the beloved another. Both are parts of a whole,
and even when emotionally one may be feeling neutral or
even annoyed by the other, that unity exists and binds one
together with the other. It is compounded by a wealth of
shared things: sexual sharing, shared experiences and
memories and hopes, possibly children. In essence it is a
deep and unquestioning acceptance of the beloved as he or
she really and truly is. It has been suggested that the nakedness of sexual love—and, after all, at its culmination sexual
love demands of us that we shall be naked together—the
nakedness of sexual love points to a more profound nakedness in this deeper kind of love which I am labouring to
describe: the nakedness which reveals without fear or
embarrassment to the beloved and only to the beloved our
imperfections. Generals doff their rows of medals and
resplendent uniforms, bishops step out of their lawn and
purple—and even their underpants and vest: unashamed of
the greying hair on the chest, the little pot belly and the old
appendix scar because they know themselves to be loved
with all their imperfections; and it is not only physical
imperfections which are laid bare to the beloved and accepted
in this kind of loving. Love—love at this depth—knows very
well the quirks of temper or temperament, the limitations,
the blind spots, the weaknesses, the vices of the beloved—
and still loves, still accepts; and the corollary of this is that,
finding oneself loved and accepted, one can even begin to
accept oneself: something we all long to do, and find incom-
parably difficult.

But I used the words 'begin to accept ourselves' advisedly,
for this kind of love is not the end of all loving. There

remain areas beyond it left to be explored, and if we fail to explore them, this kind of love can—not die—but reach a state of inanition, stop growing, and go a little flat like beer too long opened. Though this need not happen and often doesn't, it is the fate of many thoroughly good marriages; the marriages of those who have settled for what they have got, so to speak, and in settling for a static thing have begun to find it losing its savour. But there have always been people who have known other categories of love, often through darkness and pain, exploring larger areas of human consciousness, and encountering there a love more lasting, deeper, and infinitely more mysterious. I am speaking of what men have called the love of God; and it is incredibly difficult to speak of, though one of the impressive facts about it is that so many people have been forced to speak of it in much the same kind of language by the very nature of their experience of it. It is experienced as gift, they say; not as prize gained by effort, nor as reward earned, let alone as result of human talent inherited, discovered, and developed. Though it is discovered within the consciousness, it is experienced as a gift to that consciousness from without itself. It is experienced, too—and this must be said—as being beyond rationality. To know it, we must, as Jung insisted in a slightly different context, be prepared to take off our clothes of conventional logical thinking, of guidance by the intellect alone. Because of this, its reality can be, and often is, questioned, doubted, pooh-poohed or perhaps—more politely but none the less sceptically—explained away in terms of a psychological phenomenon alone; but only by those who have not known it. Of course, it is a psychological phenomenon: an occurrence within the psyche. So is one's love for a girl and one's experience of her love for us. But it is also and precisely an experience of an encounter within the psyche of an outer mystery and an inner mystery: a calling of like to like, deep to deep, and a marriage of the two. To those who have known it, its reality cannot be doubted. It isn't simply real. It *is* the reality, the discovery of reality, the breaking through for the first time into a dimension of reality hitherto only vaguely glimpsed. It results in a kind of inner integration, a unifying of the self, both as the self and with God; and it expresses itself in a vision of all things wrapped, enfolded and united in love: a vision of things without contradiction. 'All things shall be well, and all manner of things shall be well.' One does not keep the vision all the time; but it does remain perpetually there just below the threshold of consciousness, ready to break through again and again, irradiating suffering and joy, poverty and riches, and, above all, men and women with a new significance: the significance of being infinitely lovable. Paul knew it rather well. 'I know a man in Christ, fourteen years ago (whether in the body, I know not; or whether out of the body, I know not; God knoweth), such a one caught up ...' John knew how to live with it. 'Beloved, let us love one another; for love is of God; and everyone that loveth is begotten of God, and knoweth God.' But one does not need to be a Paul or a John to know the love of God; peasants have known it, poets have known it, princes have known it; rich man, poor man, beggar man, thief, have known it. It is open to all, there for all, free to all. Curiously, I believe that many are aware in their restlessness—their feeling of unfinishedness—of its possibility. They experience it as the absence of something needed for their own completion. Perhaps this is particularly so of people of your sort of age: people whom time and business have not yet wholly blunted or partly atrophied, hippies, drug addicts, and so on.

How do you find it? You don't. It is sheer gift. How do you avoid putting yourself out of reach of it? That can be answered only inadequately in the time available, for there are many ways of putting yourself out of reach of the love of God: or, rather, out of reach of becoming aware of the love of God. No man is out of reach of God himself. Some men don't want to know the love of God. They are fine without it, they think. 'I'm all right, Jack.' Some know in advance that it does not exist, because it cannot exist. It is hooey. Some are simply too busy with other things; and, of course, if those things happen to be Jew-baiting, nigger-baiting, Paki-bashing, queer-bashing, or even less violent and obvious forms of sin, the love of God is unlikely to invade such busy lives. I could go on for a long time listing ways in which people can and do protect themselves from encountering the love of God; but I won't. You can all make your own lists easily enough. Instead, I shall finish by trying to say something about the one way, as I believe, in which a man can surely put himself within reach of experiencing the love of God: the one way of opening himself to it. Appropriately, this brings me back for the last time to nakedness, this time to the ultimate nakedness, to the nakedness of the man who, poor in spirit, pride gone, illusions gone, sees himself for what he is in all his bankruptcy, without a cherished rag or a tattered lie left with which to cover his ruins, and, because he has no alternative, accepts. From such naked self-knowledge most of us will do anything to protect ourselves and will spend a lifetime of frantic and hysterical flight. 'Blessed are the poor in spirit' has always been a most unpopular saying. But to those who do not or cannot run away, into their naked self-knowledge the love of God does indeed come; as it came to one of the thieves crucified with Christ, to the tart who washed his feet with her tears and dried them with her hair, to Paul on the Damascus Road; to those who, going through the vale of misery, use it for a well: and the pools are filled with water. I have seen it filling the lives of old Jews with memories stretching back to Buchenwald and Dachau, of secretaries in bed-sits in the Bayswater Road, of little old loves waiting to die in reduced circumstances, of Africans whose absolute simplicity of heart has shamed me, of scientists astonished to have discovered it, and of a boy of twenty-three dying three weeks after his wedding while his teenage wife held his hand.

These are the people who have overcome the world. These are the people who know the peace of which Christ spoke when he said, 'Peace I leave with you, my peace I give unto you: not as the world giveth, give I unto you.' All can cry with Paul, 'Who, then, shall separate us from the love of Christ? Shall tribulation, or anguish, or persecution, or famine, or nakedness or peril or sword? ... Nay, in all these things we are more than conquerors through him that loved us. For I am persuaded that neither death, nor life, nor angels, nor principalities, nor things present, nor things to come, nor powers, nor height, nor depth, nor any other creature, shall be able to separate us from the love of God, which is in Christ Jesus our Lord.' I, too, am persuaded. I hope some of you are.

CHAPTER SIX

CAN MANKIND SURVIVE?

An unscripted discussion between Lord RITCHIE-CALDER
and Bishop HUGH MONTEFIORE

H.M.: The first question I would like to put to you is whether mankind faces a crisis at the moment and whether it is a really serious one?

R.-C.: Yes, I think it is a very serious question and the question is whether man will survive his own present mistakes and the systematic destruction of his living space.

H.M.: Now would you like to open up about what this crisis consists? Quite apart from the dangers of nuclear warfare (which I think we'd all agree is a great danger for man's survival), what about man's living space?

R.-C.: Well, if mankind does not veto the evolution of his own species by nuclear cataclysm, then the greatest problem which confronts us is overpopulation. I don't think anyone can deny the seriousness of this problem, an increase of population which will have doubled itself by the end of this century. I'd like you to realise what this means. It has taken something like a quarter of a million years for man and his missus to produce a population of 3,600 million. In the next thirty years *homo sapiens* will have doubled that figure, and there is very little which can in fact prevent that figure being 7,000 million. I say that despite the fact that many of us are very active propagating the whole question of family planning and birth control. I cannot see that you can have death control unless you have birth control; that is to say, unless you can somehow produce an equilibrium of some kind between deaths and births. It's a very difficult problem to encourage family planning throughout the entire world, but even if we do there are two factors that operate in the equation. One is that, while we are reducing the birth rate (as they have done in Japan, they have succeeded in halving it), the population still increases. The reason is the increase of the span of life. More people are surviving, more and more mouths are to be fed—180,000 more every day. In fact it is like, shall we say, Martians invading us and living off the land without ration books.

H.M.: Tell me, do you see this is a purely technical problem of birth control or a problem of underlying attitudes about the number of children that people want, especially people in less sophisticated cultures?

R.-C.: It is curious how little we do know about the processes of human reproduction considering how long it has been going on! Now it is very difficult, if you are looking at the problem throughout the world, to alter people's attitudes, their profound religious convictions and also their natural ignorance about world population as a whole. You cannot order people by edict not to reproduce. You cannot even restrict or restrain families by edict. You are not going to persuade anybody, for example, in India not to have more children because their government says so. You are not going to persuade people in under-developed countries not to have children because the global total is becoming so formidable. What you are talking about is something which is extremely intimate and extremely sensitive in every sense of the word, and quite rightly so. After all, this is the fountain origin of life; and therefore what we are trying to do is to get through not just to governments (most governments recognise now that their own material development is entirely mopped up by their multiplying survival rate), but by getting through to the people and indeed almost to the individual parents themselves. I have given a slogan to the International Planning Association. I think it's rather too sophisticated, but nevertheless it's true: 'We keep children alive.' I say that with insight and experience because I have travelled on this and similar problems something like two and a half million miles in the last twenty years and I have seen the nature of the problems actually on the spot in villages everywhere in the world; and it is true that parents today, mothers particularly, do not want to have so many children. Certainly they don't want their children to die. Now you must convince them that today by medical practice and so forth we can keep children alive, so that parents in India or Burma or in Indonesia and so on will not have to have fifteen children merely to have the possibility of five surviving.

H.M.: And do we need to redouble our efforts, do you think?

R.-C.: We need to redouble our efforts both in family planning, but above all in providing the means to feed the population of A.D. 2000. At the moment two-thirds of the people in the world are not getting food adequate to human well-being. Something like 300 million people in the world are living in a state of chronic famine. But we have got not only in the next thirty years to double the production of food, we have got also to produce the quality of food, the proteins, vitamins and so on, without which human well-being cannot be produced.

H.M.: I don't think we can go into the question of food production tonight in any detail. As someone who has been very concerned with this and has travelled about a lot, do you think it possible that when the world by the year 2000 reaches 7,000 million, that those 7,000 million can be adequately fed?

R.-C.: I believe we can adequately feed them. This is not just a question of knowledge (though we would like a great deal more knowledge which might accelerate the process), this is a question of intention. If the governments of the world and the scientists of the world and everybody else were to decide that this is the greatest problem directly for the lives of people (and it is), then I say categorically: if we'd spent forty million dollars on this problem instead of putting a man on the moon we could have cracked this problem, and could still crack it.

H.M.: But feeding people is only one aspect of the problem of overpopulation. Urbanisation and destruction of the environment is being brought about by an increasing population coupled with increasing technological knowledge. It is this, surely, that is the most serious problem for mankind?

R.-C.: Well, if we are asking 'Can mankind survive?', then we are asking what are the conditions under which man can survive and whether the living space, the biosphere, on which our whole existence depends can sustain man. How many people can we sustain and what are the conditions under which we can sustain them? The biggest problem, apart from feeding, is urbanisation. We have now got the idea of ecumenopolis. This has nothing to do with 'ecumenical': it is a world city in which the built-up area will stretch from here to its eastern suburbs in Bangkok. The west side of ecumenopolis has already happened. We now have in America the complete acceptance of 'Boswash'—a city which is going to stretch from Boston to Washington. We have another one stretching from Chicago to New Orleans; another one which I have called 'San-San' stretching from San Diego to San Francisco, a thousand miles. These cities will go on growing and spreading ulcerously—without control—and more and more people will be living in them. It's reckoned that in fifty years the entire population of the world will be living in cities. Now let's contemplate that—or perhaps you don't want to. The conditions under which people will be living would be those of factory farming. You would have tenements above ground, tenements below ground, the best methods which the scientific engineers can evolve so that a nutrient is supplied up to the thirty-sixth floor and the excrement and sewage is disposed of. This is the prospect; factory farming with battery-fed people without any consideration of amenities or of the quality of life. Take India. Calcutta is a city of six and a half million, of which three-quarters are living in squatters' conditions with no piped water supply, no proper sewage, no proper means of work or decent housing; and I was warning the Indians in Calcutta that within twenty-five years they would have in India, by the present trend, five cities with populations of sixty million each, six times as big as greater London. Well, I've given up predicting, because they begin to plan for your predictions, they don't realise that you are warning them against something. So I now prognose on the principle of the good doctor who doesn't say, except in novelettes, 'You've only got six months to live.' He says, 'If you don't do so and so, you'll only have a short time to live.' Therefore what we are talking about here is the means by which we can prevent this kind of horror. When I got to the U.S.A. a few months later, I found that the Indians through the

American Aid Programme had made a contract with the University of Michigan to plan a city of 60 million just north of Bombay; and I tried to stop it. I got into touch with the Joint Planning Commission in India and I asked, 'How many mental hospitals are you going to have in a city of sixty million?' The conditions of that city would drive people mad! I thought I'd stopped it until I went back to America the other day and found that the experts were so slide-rule happy they were then working on a city of 600 million people.

H.M.: I take it that you would agree that *homo sapiens* couldn't survive under those kinds of conditions? It would be death to the human spirit in the end?

R.-C.: Certainly *homo sapiens* couldn't survive. He'd go insane. He would become insipiens! Certainly nothing that we know of civilisation and culture could survive. It would be in fact the struggle simply to exist, there would be no quality of life in these conditions.

H.M.: Do you think that living under these conditions is likely to stir up feelings of aggression and so on?

R.-C.: Definitely. If you put animals in zoos, they become almost as aggressive as human beings, and you produce what doesn't exist in the animal kingdom, the destruction of their own species. No species destroys itself. They are the predators of other species, but I don't know any species in wild life that destroys its own species, and certainly in terms of the animals on which it preys, it never kills off its source of life. But in zoo conditions these animals become the tyrants, the bullies, the murderers and the slayers of their own kind. And in human terms this will happen. We've gone a long way already on this with *lebensraum* and so on. The struggle for somebody else's territory has been with us for quite a while. This will produce the most fantastic stresses on the whole structure of mankind and certainly it will destroy all possibilities of peace. If we do not reduce this disparity which we already have between the rich and the poor, the prosperous developed countries and the impoverished developing countries, then that will tear the world apart. If we don't do something about the conditions of life in American ghettos and so on, that will tear America apart. We are now confronted with this struggle between those who have and those who have not; and I'm not just using that in an old glib sense. This is really a basic struggle in which people may literally destroy life itself. And this is something about which we have got to be very sensitive because it does not lend itself to rational examination. In this situation of urbanisation and competition for food and so on, all the emotions which we don't fully understand are involved; and that is something that we have not fully grasped.

H.M.: We haven't yet talked about the effect of all this growing population together with a rising standard of living and the explosion of technological know-how—the effect all this is having on the creation of dereliction and destruction of wilderness, and on the pollution of the air and the sea and the soil. Our need for power increases exponentially. What about the exhaustion of raw materials and the disposal of nuclear waste?

R.-C.: Well, we are in fact creating artificial conditions for mankind, and let's be clear about this—the whole history of *homo sapiens* has been a struggle with his environment. But now we regard the extravagant use of materials as necessary. I've no quarrel with satisfying human needs, even in the technological sense. What I am very alarmed about in this whole ecological problem is that we are savagely brutalising nature. We are taking more and more out of nature in terms of the lithosphere, and in terms of the carbon from the primeval forests of hundreds of millions of years ago. We take that out, we belch it out in the form of soot or diesel fumes; and we're creating an imbalance in the environment of carbon itself. And we are gradually building up more than a possibility that in thirty years time the temperature of the earth will have been altered very considerably. We are not only altering our immediate environment and destroying ourselves with what we breath in and drink but we are in fact embracing the whole world in a new set of conditions which can restrict the capacity of the earth to deal with the pollution which we are introducing into it. Now this is savagery and selfishness. It's being created largely by artificial demand. All our technology of which we are so proud and the gadgetry in which we take so much infantile satisfaction, is in fact the creation of artificial needs. Television and the radio which were the luxuries of yesterday have now become necessities. People are making more and more demands, they are being satisfied with built-in obsolescence (to make sure that they buy another set in two years time, and so on) with the result that we are creating the most fantastic waste of our resources; and the subsequent effect of that waste is the destruction of resources.

H.M.: Now do you think that built-in obsolescence and the artificial creation of need is simply the result of the capitalist system in which a greater and greater consumption is a built-in need? To what extent do you think it is inevitable in any system?

R.-C.: It's a result of what used to be called the capitalist system. It is strange (and I speak now as a socialist) how other more primitive peoples with more primitive ideas of society begin to acquire this greed for materials. The capitalist system in its technological extravagance and its techniques has in fact created these demands, but it also has created a great deal of imitation in countries which are not capitalist. So we are looking now at a phenomenon of the second half of the 20th century in which the mere spread of communications, with the awareness of people everywhere that certain things are happening and that certain things are desirable, is one of the biggest factors. As I say, I have travelled a long way, and there is not one place in the world where the awareness of change both in the political and material sense hasn't got through. If you are the Americans or the British or if you are even the Russians boasting of their great achievements in space, you are telling the impoverished people of the world that you have the capacity to do this. And they say, 'Why don't you do this for us?' So by this 'vainglorious' advertising on a world scale you have created a tremendous sense of frustration and you are producing with it the elements of discord. People are very susceptible to advertising and therefore we have created this artificial demand. There is no more insidious television slogan than 'Don't forget the fruit gums, Mum', because what you are doing is creating, through young people, through the dispossessed or the deprived, a demand for things. Now this is a very serious problem because it is introducing into the system not only the fact of obsolescence without which the system cannot survive (if your vacuum cleaner went on working indefinitely the vacuum cleaner people would be in a bad way, if your lamps went on working more than 1,000 hours the lamp people would be in a bad way) but also a built-in demand for more.

H.M.: I want to take you now to pollution. You yourself said there was a great danger of using carbons with a resulting build-up of temperature. Is there an alternative? What about nuclear waste if we use nuclear fuel? Do you think that the great problems of pollution could be solved if we were prepared to spend the money in solving them?

R.-C.: Pollution is a crime compounded by avarice and ignorance. Exploiters go out and they create these conditions through sheer greed. That is the biggest factor in pollution. The second one is ignorance. We are ignorant about the methods by which we can prevent it. I have got very simple answers. Make every man (and I think you could almost find biblical justification for this) who creates the condition of pollution accept the responsibilities. If you have a car, then the company who made it should be eventually responsible for disposing of it. The chemical industry that produces fumes or effluents should be made responsible for making the fumes and effluents safe. At the moment what happens is that they go on exploiting these processes, injecting them into our atmosphere and our environment; and then society (that's you and me) pick up the bills in the form of either health services or public health measures, indeed in the reconstruction of the environment. And may I say very simply here (because I get so frightened sometimes) that conditions in this country are now beginning to respond to anti-pollution. We are getting an awareness and we are getting a sense of public responsibility in the great corporations. But it still stands that they should be held to be guilty until they can prove their processes innocent. I don't believe that any man should be allowed to introduce something new into the environment until he has satisfied us that it will be harmless.

H.M.: I take it that you would agree that pollution is no longer a localised problem and unless we have world agreement on many matters *homo sapiens* probably is sunk?

R.-C.: Well, it is no longer a local problem. There is no

confined midden heap in the world now. That is to say, all your pollutions finally find their way into the sea. You know the story of the Rhine, the Baltic has become practically a cesspool, Lake Erie in the Great Lakes is dead; but in addition all our great oceans which seem limitless are now becoming dangerously polluted in areas where we ourselves are at hazard. That is to say, the whole of the food-sustaining layers of the sea are becoming affected. This is international; and there is no international law at the moment to confine it. In dealing with the disposal of atomic waste and so forth we are just slap-happy. This is very much an international problem. In 1972, perhaps rather late, we are having the great international United Nations Convention promoted by the Swedes (who incidentally have contributed quite a lot of pickling acids into the Baltic by this time). If we don't control all this, it ultimately means the destruction of the means of survival for mankind.

H.M.: Can we perhaps move on from there to what seems to me to lie near the heart of this matter? From what you say it seems to me that man's hope of survival depends, certainly on the level of future population, secondly on the knowledge of what effect he is having on his environment, and thirdly, on his will to put things right even if this means that he cannot indulge himself in all the material possessions which he may regard today as necessities. This to me raises the basic question of how on earth humanity is to find the will to put this right. Perhaps this is a point at which you and I, who would probably agree with everything which has been said up to this point, might diverge. I want you to have the last word, Lord Ritchie-Calder; and for that reason I am going to say now how I see it. I see man as made in God's image and therefore responsible to God for what he does; having stewardship over all the natural world and therefore responsible to God for the way in which he uses it and also having an obligation to use his stewardship so that posterity will be no worse off than we are now. As I see it, I can't believe that man can find the will to put things right unless he sees this world in the perspective of eternity—so that he doesn't put all his money on this world—and secondly, unless he sees himself as responsible to God and receiving from God grace and power to put into action that which his selfishness at the moment forbids him from doing and often even from thinking about. This is why to me in this question 'Can man survive?' the question of belief in God is terribly important. You may well say (and I shall listen with great respect to what you will say), that on a humanist basis you think that there is a good chance of man's survival. I should like you to look if you would in the closing minutes at these underlying attitudes of moral behaviour and how you think man can find the will to solve them.

R.-C.: Thank you very much. This is a challenge to the humanist (and I would point out that the humanist is not basically in conflict with Christianity or with any other form of religion). My position is very simple. I am a scientific humanist. I believe that (what is almost a resonance of what has been said) man is perfectible; and indeed if I didn't believe man was capable of solving his problems I don't think I could go on. But I am talking about men and people; and I did write a book called *After the Seventh Day*—the world that man himself created—and I may say that I have tackled all these problems that you are discussing tonight. I started from the position that man in his stewardship is responsible to other men throughout the world, that all of us have got a responsibility to others in this world, that we have an absolute obligation to share our knowledge and our skills and our sympathy and that in the community of mankind you can in fact find the answers. Let me say that I am an agnostic, not an atheist. I haven't got the impertinence to say that there is no God. All I say is that I do not know that God exists. In the urgency, and the width and the breadth and the depth which this problem demands, if you can show to me that the power of prayer could do something where the power of persuasion has so far not succeeded, then I will perhaps change my mind. I don't see it. I said on a television programme that because I was so fully aware of the urgent necessities of this problem, I could not afford the luxury of God. This caused amongst a lot of very dear friends of mine who tolerate me as an agnostic a great deal of violent reaction because they had misheard or they thought I had said, '*We* cannot afford the luxury of God.' Now I don't deny anybody the luxury of God. I just say that I in the urgency of my problem of having to do something about it, cannot in fact afford the luxury of God. I cannot find the answers in prayer or in any escape that one can have by passing on responsibility to God. I see it as a manifest responsibility of all the people who are making the mistakes, of all the people who are perpetuating their ignorance because they refuse to see what has to be done, of all the politicians I've got to work with, of all the statesmen in the world who have got to be brought together to deal with this kind of thing; and I see this as an urgent practical and definitely a very human problem.

H.M.: Thank you very much. This is a larger problem than any kind of narrow ecclesiasticism. When I look at the history of the Christian Church in this particular field there is very much of which to be ashamed from the past; and without changing my own convictions, I very much respect what you have just said. *The problem is so urgent.* There is a vast field here for all possible co-operation with everybody who is concerned with the future of humanity. I'm sure we would agree there.

A final question which I am going to put to you, Lord Ritchie-Calder, and which I would be grateful if you will answer to the best of your ability in one word. Can mankind survive?

R.-C.: Yes.

ON CHRISTIANITY

CHAPTER SEVEN

A COURSE OF THREE ADDRESSES:

1—ON BEING HUMAN

by FR. HARRY WILLIAMS, C.R.,
formerly Dean of Trinity College, Cambridge

It is typical of your Vicar's wisdom and understanding that he should ask for a sermon on being human as we are approaching the middle of the Lent Term—a time when our spirits tend to flag a bit and we begin to ask ourselves what on earth we are doing here and who or what we are anyway. We are human enough to feel a little inhuman at this time of year, not, I mean, in our attitude to others but in the doubts we have about ourselves. Those doubts disguise themselves as misgivings about our ability to make the grade—either academically or socially or sexually or professionally. But beneath that disguise the persecuting question-mark is really levelled at us as people. Am I substandard as a human person? Don't I lack some essential element which most other people seem to have? Am I, in short, all there?

It is when feelings of that kind begin to worry us, or in other words, when we feel slightly depressed, that we recognise the importance of trying to discover what being human in fact means. Once you begin thinking about it, it is curious how difficult being human is to describe. Here we are, human ourselves, having lived with other humans all our lives. It ought to be easy enough to set out the special characteristics of our human condition. Yet when we attempt to do so, we find the reality we are struggling to describe is so fantastically subtle and complex that our attempted description seems flat and lifeless, somehow leaving out more than it includes. Say, for instance, in the language of Christian orthodoxy, that man is made in the image of God and you have forgotten that gods are invariably made in the image of the men who worship them. Or say that man is a rational animal and you have forgotten that man's reason is little more than the servant of his desire. Or use the statis-

tical methods of sociological research and you find that in
the West the average family consist of 2·5 children. Or try
to elicit the secret of human identity from the tenets of
psychoanalytic orthodoxy and you find that man is an incar-
nation of the Oedipus complex. The trouble is that when
you combine these various answers they don't add up to a
coherent whole. They remain a jumble of unrelated bits and
pieces. Humanity has a tiresome habit of slipping through
the categories used to describe it, and perkily thumb-nosing
the descriptions it has evaded. Our very use of the adjective human is a good example. It can indicate praise—'He is
a very human person.' It can also indicate a state of affairs far
from praiseworthy—'He's only human after all.'

I think there is only one way out of this maze. What else
can any of us do but examine the depths of his own inner
experience? That, at any rate, is what I intend to do this
evening. What I feel and think about myself will not coincide
exactly with what any of you feel and think about yourselves.
But I am confident that there will be common ground enough
for the exercise not to be a complete waste of time. If you
find much of what I say untrue to your own experience, then
quite a lot of what you are will have been brought to your
notice, and that, after all, is what we are trying to get at.
Nobody can tell you what you are, as so much information.
You have to discover it for yourself, from the living actual
human being which is you. And that is what you will be
doing both when you find your experience similar to mine
and when you find it different.

In my own experience being human consists above all in
my capacity to accept. And it is upon this capacity to accept
that I want now to dwell. You will naturally want to ask
at once—to accept what? But I intend for the moment to
postpone consideration of what as humans we find ourselves accepting, in order to concentrate first upon the act
or process of accepting itself. What is this most human of all
activities and how can it be described?

First of all let us get rid of the notion that accepting
equals passivity, as in the phrase 'the passive acceptance of
so and so'. If by some mistake you find yourself given lodg-
ings in a gas-works, you may be too lazy to do anything
about it. But it does not mean that you have accepted the
smell and noise of your environment. You are in fact too

lazy to do anything but put up with your own inner non-acceptance of the smell and noise. Passivity means putting up with your own inner non-acceptance of anything. Activity, on the other hand, means either changing what you can't accept into something which you can (that's too obvious to need enlarging upon), or, and from the point of view of this discussion much more important, learning to accept what previously you did not accept. If, for instance, this evening I were to have an accident which made me permanently blind, at first I should merely put up with my blindness, resign myself to my not accepting it. But in time I might actually accept it as a way of life and thereby discover that it brought possibilities of which I was formerly unaware. This learning to accept my blindness would have nothing to do with being passive. It would be an activity of the highest order, and uniquely human.

But granted that accepting is the exact opposite of passivity, can it be called uniquely human? After all, is not the whole story of evolution concerned with the adaptation of species to their environment, and do not laboratory experiments with animals demonstrate their capacity to adjust themselves to changing situations? Well, of course. No claim is being made that there was a break in continuity between man and his animal ancestors. But that doesn't mean that what is found embryonically in animals is not found in a unique degree in man. Instinctive adjustment to environment in animals may sometimes border on something which looks like the first beginnings of what in man is a voluntary act of acceptance. That is what we should expect. The difference lies in the degree in which the dominating factor is either a matter of instinct or a matter of voluntary choice. After all, there are hundreds of occasions when humans instinctively adjust themselves to new environments as when we drop an object which is too hot for us to hold, or when, going into a cinema, our eyes adjust themselves to the darkness so that we can see the seats which at first were invisible, or when we tense up when danger looms, gathering our physical strength to strike the theatening assailant. But this is a different experience altogether from that of man who gradually learns to accept his blindness.

Thus the points made still stand—accepting is an activity and in its developed form is uniquely human.

Now comes what is the most difficult element of experience to describe. Accepting, we have said, is a matter of voluntary choice. And once we begin talking about voluntary choice there is a terrible danger of over-simplification. At first glance choosing seems such an obvious and straightforward matter. But to assume that it always or often is is one of the cruellest things we can do either to ourselves or to others. Voluntary choice is in important matters an immensely complex affair. To illustrate its complexity I shall describe people in various situations making the voluntary choice to accept.

In superficial matters it is of course straightforward enough. I decide to accept John's invitation to his party. I like him. I enjoy the society of his friends. And there is always plenty to drink. No trouble there. My director of studies, however, has told me to attend the lectures of Professor X which are at nine in the morning, and his lectures are indeed generally recognised as interesting and valuable. Choosing to attend them is from one point of view as simple a matter as choosing to attend John's party. I set my alarm clock, get up when it rings, and bicycle to the lecture room. All these things are within the scope of what is generally called my will power. So far, so good. But at this point my will power has done all it can, and some other process takes over. I find that the professor's lecture is indeed extremely interesting, and my acceptance of its value has nothing to do with will power at all. Some deeper and more comprehensive aspects of my being are brought into play. I forget myself entirely as my interest is caught up in the theme the professor is expounding. The fifty minutes of his lecture seem like ten. Here you have a situation where will power is not operating and yet acceptance is entirely voluntary. The professor is not a hypnotist. Nor has some super academic authority insisted that we should be interested. Our acceptance of the lecture's value is spontaneous. And if at the end of the fifty minutes we feel more alive than before, that is because it has enabled us to experience some new dimension of freedom generally inaccessible.

But now suppose that things don't go quite so well. I get myself to the lecture room, but it is in the face of some undefined sense of grievance at my being expected to attend. My chief concern at the moment is with Betty's going out to

dinner last night with John, or with the need to find the
money to pay my college bill. Instead of having the time
to ponder on these matters, some slave-driver within myself
has forced me to attend the lecture. The will power which
has brought me to the lecture room continues to function in
the effort to concentrate upon what the professor is saying.
But the act of concentrating takes up so much of my attention that little is left for the actual content of the lecture.
Far from feeling free, it is as though I were bound hand and
foot. I am all but incapable of accepting anything the professor says. We are now in an area of great mystery where a
choice is made which has nothing to do with will power. In
some obscure part of my being I choose whether to let the
undefined sense of grievance predominate so that I am closed
up against what the professor says, or whether to open myself
to his ideas so that I gradually find myself accepting them
without the grim determination to do so. This is a real choice
leading to a voluntary non-acceptance or acceptance. But it
is not a simple choice like deciding to bicycle to the lecture
room.

It is the kind of choice which has to be made by all artists
in every medium. You can't write a poem or compose a
symphony by the brute force of will power. The muses
simply won't obey the military word of command. Yet the
artist has to choose whether to cultivate his inspiration or
whether to neglect it. That inspiration is frightening, taxing,
daunting. It is easier therefore for him to occupy himself
with routine work, persuading himself that he is too busy to
listen to the voices which are struggling within him to be
heard. But then, at some point, he will have the courage to
stop and listen to what they have to say in spite of the
turmoil which they will bring. And it is from that choice to
accept what within him is demanding expression, it is from
that choice, that the work of creation is achieved.

An experience more commonly shared is the decision to
make or accept a proposal of marriage. Even in the most
despotic and totalitarian of states a man is free to propose
to the woman he loves and the woman is free to accept or
refuse him. The proposal and response are entirely voluntary.
Yet it is in no obvious sense that we are exercising our freedom to choose. For choice here means acknowledging and
submitting to some compelling power within us which can

no longer be gainsaid. Yet if the man proposes and the woman accepts, submission to this compelling power within is experienced as one of the highest forms of freedom.

Let me now recapitulate. Being human consists above all in the capacity to accept. This capacity in its developed form is seen to be quite different from that instinctive adjustment to environment which man shares with the other animals. It is an activity—the opposite of passive acquiescence. And it proceeds from voluntary choice, although this voluntary choice is of so deep and subtle a nature that it quickly passes beyond the range of what we call will power.

But if being human consists in this capacity to accept, what then is it that as humans we are called upon to accept?

The answer is so simple that in a sense it sounds ridiculous. What confronts us with the demand for acceptance is what we are. It is the capacity to accept what I am which makes me human. To the degree in which I am unable to accept what I am, to that degree am I less than fully human. To the degree in which I am able so to accept myself, to that degree am I coming into my human heritage.

So, for instance, some people find it hard to accept the fact of their animal nature. The classic example of this was the fanatical opposition shown by many Victorian Christians to the discovery of how man evolved from animal ancestors. That controversy is now long dead. But what is accepted as a scientific fact can be rejected when it becomes a matter of private and personal involvement. Not a few people, for instance, are worried because they think, as they put it, that they are over-sexed. What in fact it means is that they cannot accept the inevitability in an animal nature of strong upsurges of instinct. And what makes them less than human is not the strength of the instinct but their incapacity to accept it as inevitable. Others reject their animal nature by overtaxing their physical resources and trying to live as though they didn't need sleep and food and rest. It annoys them that they feel tired and worn out or that they have to stop what they are doing in order to have a meal. Here again, it is not their physical needs which make them less than human but their refusal to accept the necessity of those needs. Others again are appalled by the violence of their aggressive feelings. Those feelings are called forth by a threat, real or imaginary. And unless that instinct to preserve ourselves by overcoming

the assailant were part and parcel of our nature we should
not have survived as a species in the evolutionary process.
Of course what threatens us now is not an animal looking
for a meal but the clever acquaintance bent on showing by
his wit that we are intellectually negligible, but our instinctive response to danger is the same. And we have to learn
to accept the consequent aggression in ourselves as both
healthy and inevitable.

As possessing an animal nature we have to accept ourselves as belonging to a species. What we have also to accept is
our unique individuality, that I am I myself, the only me,
who is what he is because of countless conditioning factors
which go back to the dawn of time. But to see what is
meant we need take back those conditioning factors no further
than a generation. My parents were people of this sort. I
have inherited something of their physique and their temperament, and being brought up in the atmosphere which
their presence generated has left its inevitable marks upon
me, either by way of imitation or of reaction. Their circumstances were such and such. Their interests and outlook on
life were so and so. We lived in that sort of place and I
was sent to that sort of school, and my uncles, aunts and
cousins did and do this and that. These conditioning factors
have helped to make me what I now am, with this degree
of good or bad looks, this degree of intelligence and sensi-
tivity, this degree of confidence, and so on and so on. It is
useless for us to wish that we were different people who
had different kinds of parents and who came from different
backgrounds—more loving, more secure, less narrow-minded
and the rest. Our particular past is stamped upon us from
head to foot. Many people spend a great deal of their lives
resenting the conditioning factors which have made them
the only Richard or the only Mary of their kind in existence.
But one of the main challenges which confronts every human
being is the choice to accept the past which he finds imposed
upon him and which has made him unlike anybody else.
Failure so to accept leads to sterile and undirected protest.
It is a good and noble thing to protest against what we
believe to be morally wrong in the structure of society. Without such protest, humanity would wither away. But we must
be very careful to make sure that we are not in the last
resort protesting for protesting's sake. For that would indicate

that we have failed in one of the most importance challenges
of human life—to accept ourselves as the products of our
particular pasts. When we thus fail to accept what the past
has made us, the defiance which we appear to throw at the
world is no more than a disguise for the defiance we are
throwing at ourselves. To me the supreme example in this
century of such failure to accept is Adolf Hitler. The whole
diabolical apparatus of Nazi Germany, with its murder of
millions of Jews, its superstition of the Aryan super-race, its
attempt to dominate the world, was the product of somebody who could not accept what his past had made him, and
who played upon and blew up to gigantic proportions the
same tendency to non-acceptance of themselves in the German people. The result was the staging of a horrific and
ruthless charade designed to persuade Hitler and his followers
that they were not what in fact they were, to persuade them
that they were super-men and not people whose past had
left them with slightly more than average feelings of
inferiority. That illusion was finally shattered in the bunker
in Berlin. And as a positive force the Nazi movement had
and has no future, apart from sporadic isolated outbursts here
and there which amount to nothing. By way of contrast, consider Lenin. The Kremlin, it is true, has consistently been
unfaithful to its first leader, but the movement he
inaugurated is still alive in Russia as the readiness of intelligent Russians to go to prison for their convictions has shown,
and Communism is still the dominating force in vast areas
of the world. Lenin changed the course of history as Hitler
did not, and he was able to do so because he accepted himself as the product of his past environment. What largely
adverse conditioning factors had made him, he used as his
supreme opportunity.

Hitler's devilish charade was an attempted antidote for
doubt and anxiety. This reminds us that we cannot be human
unless we are willing to accept doubt and anxiety. I say this
here in case I have given the impression that if we are able
to accept our past, then life will be perpetually serene and
unclouded. It won't. From time to time we shall doubt our
capacities, we shall be uncertain whether we can keep it up,
we shall be anxious about the future, we shall wonder whether
life has much meaning or value after all, we shall feel that
nobody likes us much, we shall think of ourselves as one big

promise of failure, we shall suspect that no woman will ever love us because there will always be another man she loves more, we shall in short feel sub-human. To be human is precisely to be vulnerable to this sort of inner attack. If we regard it as intolerable, outrageous or even unusual that we should have occasionally to undergo suffering of this kind, then we shall only make it worse. Whatever you pretend to your friends, don't pretend to yourself that you are not in fact feeling what you are. If you accept these attacks or doubt as an inevitable part of being human, their hold on you will grow weaker and you will find yourself passing through them as through a temporary storm. If you don't accept them it means that you will worry about them, and then their hold on you will grow stronger. And if their hold on you is too persistent, you may find yourself putting on your own charade for your own benefit, building up a ficti-tious you who is tough, or heartless, or full of fun, or oozing with bonhomie or sensibly never ruffled, as the case may be. If you can come to believe that this stage-prop of painted cardboard was in fact your true self, then your capacity to accept would dwindle to insignificance. You would be hardly human.

That is all I have to say tonight. I have told you what in my own experience being human means—the capacity to accept, how the act or process of accepting is no simple matter because, although voluntary, it quickly passes beyond the range of your will power, and what we have to accept is what we are. On this last item, however, my range of examples has been very narrow, because I have deliberately omitted what could be called the Christian experience. But I hope to speak about that next Sunday.

CHAPTER EIGHT

A COURSE OF THREE ADDRESSES:

2—ON CHRISTIAN EXPERIENCE

by FR. HARRY WILLIAMS, C.R.,
formerly Dean of Trinity College, Cambridge

Last Sunday I said that being human consisted in my capacity to accept. I tried to describe the act or process of accepting, pointing out that although it was a matter of voluntary choice, such choosing soon passed beyond the range of will power. I then gave some examples of what as humans we find ourselves called upon to accept, deliberately omitting what belongs to specifically Christian experience. It is to that specifically Christian experience that I now turn.

It is impossible to speak of Christian experience without first speaking of Christ. The New Testament describes him as the pioneer and perfector of our faith. In him we see what being a Christian means. But he is not only the complete model of Christian life and faith. Being a Christian means sharing his identity and making it our own. It means being people in whom his life and character and power are manifest and energised. As St. Paul said, 'For me to live is Christ.' So Christian experience is not so much a matter of imitating a leader or adhering to the precepts of a founder as accepting and receiving a new quality of life—a life infinitely more profound and dynamic and meaningful than human life without Christ.

From one point of view it is difficult to speak of Christ because you can't pin him down. You can't reduce him to a neat and intellectually satisfying description. If you think you can do that, you are in danger of turning him into an idol. In the history of Christian thought and practice Christ has sometimes been cut down to the dimensions of a formula. He has been described, for instance, as though he existed to guarantee the inerrancy of the Church or to provide the emotional solution to pent-up feelings of inadequacy. We must beware of turning him into a formula of this kind. But that doesn't mean that we can't select what we believe to be the most important truths about him and describe them as best we may, so long as we realise all the time that our selection and description must of necessity be partial and inadequate.

What, then, we see in Christ is the creation of goodness and love, not by escaping from the moral ambiguities and contradictions of life in the world but by being fully involved in them. This creation of goodness through full involvement in the complications of human life was achieved at the cost of suffering and death. But this suffering and death was not the last word in the story, for they came to be seen as the very hallmarks of final and indestructible success. Or to put it in more customary language, in Christ we see God coming into human life and taking all its destructive evil upon himself. That entry into our condition and involvement in all the forces destroying life was only accomplished by the acceptance of suffering. So Christ was crucified. But death was not the final truth, for the Crucified was revealed as alive for evermore and as exercising all authority in heaven and on earth. Such in outline is what Christians call God's saving act in Christ. But it is not something of which Christians are mere spectators or to which they give the mere audience response of people in a theatre. They are caught up in the drama so that it becomes their own. In the history of Christ it is their own history that they see, or can see.

But let us now turn to the details of this inadequate description. We shall consider them under three main headings: the creation of goodness while being fully involved in the world, the cost of suffering and the achievement of victory. We shall try to show that because these three things were true of Christ they can be true also of us as Christ gives us his life as our own. But we must first note that the life which Christ gives has to be accepted, and here I make no apologies for repeating what I have already said about the act or process of accepting: that in important things while accepting remains a matter of voluntary choice, choosing in these areas of importance is so subtle and complex a process that it leaves will power behind. Remember choosing to absorb Professor X's lecture, the artist choosing to cultivate his own inspiration, choosing to ask so and so to marry you. These provide possible parallels for our choosing to accept Christ's life as our own. We can't do it as we decide to take an overcoat on a walk. That is why so much talk about deciding for Christ is superficial and unreal, as though it were little more than adding our signature to a fly-sheet or making up our minds to drink a pint of milk a day. The decision to accept Christ's life as our own is taken gradually in areas of our being of which we are far from fully aware. Yet it remains a voluntary choice because it is not done under the stress of any compulsion; it is an act or process in which our total personality is engaged; and it brings an experience of freedom which releases new energies within us.

So let us consider involvement, suffering and victory as the characteristics of Christ which by our voluntary acceptance can become our own. Christ was not born into the simple uncomplicated life of our more childish fantasies. He was born into a turbulent province of the Roman Empire in which there was a great deal of unrest—political, economic and racial. The Jews in Palestine were under the dominion of an occupying power which had little use for their ideals and no knowledge of their God. And they felt the burden of their oppression as keenly as the Czechoslovak people today. What was to be their attitude to the Romans? Here there was a considerable and fierce difference of opinion, from the Zealots at one end who wanted immediate revolution to the Sadducees at the other who practised almost complete collaboration. From the political point of view, Palestine in the first century was far from being a promising field in which to create goodness and love. Economically there were, as in the rest of the world at that time, vast differences in wealth between the rich and the poor. Indignation at the injustice of this state of affairs glows through many of the sayings of Jesus. If you examine all the references in the Gospels to riches and poverty you will see what I mean. Meanwhile, through it all, there was the persistent corruption of petty officials whose careful lining of their own pockets was notorious. Even worse than this economic jungle was racial prejudice. The Jews, St. John tells us, had no dealings with the Samaritans—to the Jews the Samaritans were the West Indians of the time, immigrants of some centuries past. The Romans in their turn thought themselves superior as a race to the Jews. Pilate's cynicism in handing Jesus over to be unjustly executed was the result of his despising the people he had been sent to govern. Wasn't the death of an obscure Jew a small price to pay for the solution of a little local difficulty?

Such was the political, economic and racial climate in which Jesus lived. He might have despaired of doing anything constructive—how insignificant he must have looked compared with the hostile forces around him. Yet he went about working for honesty in men's lives, for justice, for compassion, for healing, for forgiveness, for reconciliation, for peace. In terms of the contemporary scene he achieved very little. But by his patient and courageous continuance in well-doing, in spite of the apparent odds, he became and remains the greatest influence for good the world has even seen. When we work for honesty and justice and compassion and peace it may look as though we are achieving little. Political and economic forces bent on robbing man of his humanity continue in their daunting strength. Racial prejudice and hatred seem, if anything, on the increase. And over all lies the threat of extermination by the H-bomb. In this context it is tempting merely to cultivate our own back gardens, cut out a private life of our own and hope that with luck we may continue in it as long as our lives last. Yet it was in a context parallel, as we have seen, to this that Christ created goodness by his steadfast and absolute loyalty to its demands. And the honesty and justice and compassion and peace which he actualised in all he said and did are still with us for the healing of the world. To share his life means to work for goodness not only in the hope, but in the knowledge, that what we are thus enabled to do will not and cannot be thrown away but will remain to build up and establish mankind in truth and righteousness. The Christian experience is this knowledge that what we do, in and by the spirit of Christ, is never in vain. We can choose to give up in cynicism or despair. Or we can choose to accept Christ's healing work as our own and to accomplish it as those who know it will remain. Here I wish to add two comments. First, to work for healing and goodness we have to use our wits. How can we most effectively bring influence to bear upon the society in which we live? That will require reading, reflection, discussion and experiment. In short, it will require sweat. Secondly, involvement in this world can take as many forms as there are people. For some it will mean crusading for this or the other cause, for others it will mean the conscientious discharge of their ordinary daily work, for others again it will mean a life especially dedicated to prayer and contemplation. None of these ways is better than the other. It is simply that there are different types of endeavour suited to different types of aptitude. It is for each of us to discover to which type of endeavour he is called. Having done so, we must not despise or denigrate those whose calling is different from our own.

In the complicated and often hostile environment in which he lived, Christ created goodness. We must now pass on to notice that the cost of this creation was suffering. We know that Christ was tempted. The story of his forty days in the wilderness suggests that he was tempted to bogus, dramatic and easy answers. We know that he suffered unspeakable torment in the Garden of Gethsemane. We know that he was deserted by his friends, reviled by his countrymen and died in anguish upon the cross. By the use of our imagination we can fill in the details of his suffering, but the details are not given us in the Gospels, probably because they were not communicable. I don't want therefore to elaborate upon Christ's suffering. It is enough to know that he did suffer, to the extent to which human nature is capable of suffering. That tells us that, to create goodness in this world, suffering is inevitable. And I want to suggest ways in which this element of Christian experience can manifest in our own lives. First, there is the pain of not always, perhaps seldom, being able to perceive the results of our efforts. We must be prepared to work and not to see the goodness thereby created. Having laboured, we must be prepared for the pain of apparent frustration and non-effectiveness. It was this which was seen so clearly by St. Ignatius Loyola, when he taught his followers to pray, 'Teach us to labour and not ask for any reward save that of knowing that we do thy will.' Christ died before he saw anything whatever accomplished by his life's work. And we must be at least prepared to share with him the experience of apparent failure, because what looks like human failure is the vehicle of God's success—one of

the major scandals of Christianity which the Church down
the centuries has constantly been tempted to forget as it has
lowered the flag and striven to fight the world with its own
weapons, a course which nothing could redeem from insin-
cerity save its inherent stupidity. 'We wrestle,' said St. Paul,
'not against flesh and blood, but against cosmic powers,
against spiritual forces of evil.' Another form of pain when
we share Christ's life and create goodness may well be the
pain of division, division within our family and among our
closest friends. We must remember that Christ told us he
had come not to bring peace but a sword, to set people over
against each other. When there are deep differences of
principle within a family or among an intimate circle of
friends, it can be agonisingly difficult to bear because we
hurt the people we care for most in the tenderest area of
their affection for us. Their happiness in us, their rejoicing
over us, the sense they gave us that they were glad to be
alive because we were what we were—it was the warmth of
this loving happy approval by which we grew and lived.
Then in loyalty to some form of truth or righteousness which
constrains us we have to pull ourselves out of the circle of
their conviction and practice. It may be in some matter of
public policy. It may be in the field of private morals. It
may be concerned with religion, when we can no longer
share their beliefs or imitate their form of piety. A deep
estrangement grows up between us. And it hurts us a great
deal to hurt them. Often we try to assuage our pain by
feelings of anger or derision. But when we feel scorn and
anger towards people with whom we are intimately connected, we can be pretty certain that the scorn and anger are
antidotes to the pain of having hurt them. It's not easy to
forgive those people we've hurt.

Along with that sort of pain, there is the pain of inevitable
uncertainty. For all we can ever be is reasonably certain
that we are right. And to be reasonably certain means to be
also uncertain. Nobody can work for goodness and love without bearing the burden of doubt. The ideal we are aiming
for may be clear enough, but to *work* for an ideal involves
choosing this method rather than that, giving offence here in
order to give help there. Our choice of method is inevitably
fallible. Nothing of good would ever have been achieved
anywhere unless those who worked for it had been ready to

suffer the nagging pain of never being quite certain whether they were acting for the best.

Sometimes the suffering is more violent. When, for instance, a person is struggling to attain integrity of character, to be fully the person he has it in him to be, the process can be accompanied by a terrible amount of mental turmoil. It is a pity that when we think of psychic disturbance we invariably consider it in terms of the analogy of physical illness. When you get better after being physically ill, the *status quo* of physical health is restored. That is not true of those psychic mental disturbances from which we all suffer from time to time. They are a drive towards wholeness and integrity. They are a demand for a greater personal honesty. They are the price we have to pay for the creation of a greater goodness within ourselves. And when eventually we pass through them, we do not return to the *status quo ante*. We are greater people capable of doing greater things, able now to give to a degree which before we could not give. When therefore such disturbances come, they can be accepted as a most important element of Christian experience because they are a form of that suffering by means of which truth and goodness are being established.

To some people, as indeed to Christ himself, the suffering can be brutally physical. But there is no need to speak of that, since our contemporary world has already provided us with all too many examples of those who have been wounded and killed for righteousness sake.

If Christ gives us his life so that we may create goodness and the cost is suffering, that is not the end of the story. For the suffering is not simply something we have to put up with and bear for a season like a toothache at the weekend. Nor is it simply the inevitable concomitant of doing something worth while such as the exhaustion you feel if over a long period you work very hard. It is that certainly. But it is not only that. The suffering, if accepted in Christ and for his sake, is itself creative of good because it is the means whereby the power of God is brought to bear upon the world. This is difficult for us to understand because it is so absolutely contrary to the wisdom of this world. St. Paul, in one of the most stupendous of his affirmations declares: 'We preach Christ crucified, to the Jews a stumbling-block, to the Greeks foolishness, but to us, Christ the power of

God and the wisdom of God.' Christ's absolute success in creating goodness was achieved by means of what the world calls failure. As Professor McKinnon has recently reminded us, we misread the Gospels if we understand them as giving us a story with a happy ending. They end with happiness indeed, with more, with joy unspeakable and full of glory. But that happiness, that joy was the result not of contemplating events in an earthly light as a newspaper correspondent might do. The joy came by seeing those events in the light of what God did by means of them. For God works not through human success but through people consecrated to the purposes of his love. In the history of Christ what matters is his absolute devotion to truth, justice and love, what the New Testament calls his Father's will. It is because of that absolute devotion that he now lives and reigns eternally. In a world where falsehood, injustice and hatred are rampant, such absolute devotion to their opposites brings conflict, suffering, and death. But (and this is the real scandal to our ordinary way of thinking) the suffering and the death are the very means by which God triumphs. It is by them that God accomplishes the victory which overcomes evil. So, Christians proclaim, Christ rose from the dead. What the resurrection of Christ was in terms of newspaper reporting, it is difficult to know. But his disciples became overwhelmingly aware of their crucified master as present among them and within them, the source of limitless life and power and love and joy. In that experience they looked back on his death as the event above all others in which he achieved victory for all that was good. Perhaps we can better understand this paradox if we consider somebody in our own century who, sharing Christ's life, partook in great measure of his experience. I refer to Dietrich Bonhoeffer. What is the secret of his continuing influence? He had of course many insights into the meaning of Christian discipleship. Yet as a thinker he is very vulnerable. He often contradicts himself in his writings, so that some are able to claim him as a champion of theology without God while others claim him as a champion of God without theology. The power of Bonhoeffer is to be found only in a minor degree in what he wrote. His real power is to be found in his dedication to truth and justice which brought him into ultimate conflict with Nazi Germany. From the ordinary human point of view his life was the blackest of tragedies. Certainly it had no happy ending. He was taken out and shot within a few weeks of Germany's defeat. Yet when we now look back on what he was, how he behaved, what happened to him, what we behold is not tragedy but victory. We see in him the triumph of goodness over evil. His history, far from driving us to despair, increases our hope. Here, we are convinced, is where God was and where God won. Few of us here this evening will have to suffer so keenly or so dramatically as Bonhoeffer. But we can learn to accept our own minor sufferings as the place where God is perceived and where God is winning. When we can't see the results of our striving, when our devotion to principle leads to division among family and friends, when we are in uncertainty, when we are in a state of mental and emotional turmoil, when some great prophet and leader is done down and killed, precisely in these places we can have eyes to see God at work creating justice and honesty, compassion and love. For in us, in men and women throughout the world, Christ is still being crucified and still is he being raised from the dead. That is the very inmost heart of the Christian experience.

Christ offers you his life to make your own. If you accept, it won't make life easy. In many ways, it will make it harder. But it will give meaning to all that you do and to all that happens to you. Your total experience will be harnessed to the achievement of justice and compassion and reconciliation and peace. You can't accept Christ once for all tonight. But that voluntary choice can be made slowly over the months and over the years, for being human means having the capacity thus to accept. I know that when one thinks of what we are like—our selfishness and pettiness and meanness and narrowness, our concern for our own comfort and convenience, our wanting so frantically to climb the ladder of success—when we think of all that, it seems incredible that we could become somebody through whom healing and love flows forth to mankind. But it is always to people like us, to the undeserving poor, that Christ gives himself. And the offer is never withdrawn.

CHAPTER NINE

A COURSE OF THREE ADDRESSES:

3—ON BELONGING

by FR. HARRY WILLIAMS, C.R.,
formerly Dean of Trinity College, Cambridge

During the last two Sundays I had no time to speak much, if at all, about happiness. I don't know whether you noticed the omission, but I hope you did. For being human means being happy (it is being less than human which makes us less than happy), while to the degree in which we are willing to receive Christ's life as our own and find in him our own truest and deepest identity (which means becoming fully human), to that degree are we fully happy.

There is, of course, a true and a bogus happiness. How can they be distinguished? When you come across bogus happiness it irritates and depresses you, and irrationally you feel jealous. 'Why are they so happy when I'm not?' But when you meet true happiness it's never felt to be exclusive. There's about it a totally unselfconscious openness and givingness, which communicates itself to others and makes them feel more worthwhile. A married couple, for instance, can make you feel depressingly an outsider. That's the result of their flaunting their happiness in your face because some of it isn't real and they have to compensate themselves at your expense. On the other hand when you go into the home of a couple who are genuinely happy there's no need for them to try to share their happiness with you. It just happens. You get caught up in the truly happy atmosphere and their happiness becomes your own. The same distinction can be observed with regard to religious people. They can be terribly depressing, not to say irritating. Many religious get-togethers make me squirm and I want to announce as a hymn the notorious song from *Hair*. Now I think it's because for all their talk of Christ liberating them into happiness their happiness is to some degree bogus. When I visited monastic communities I realised that something was obvious but I couldn't make out what it was. Last June I discovered when it suddenly came to me, 'My God, they're happy.' They never told you that they were. You could feel it in the air and this meant the complete absence of religiosity. In this sense they were as non-religious as Great St. Mary's notoriously is! I remember a very old monk sitting on a garden seat and mumbling to me, 'Wonderful person, one of the greatest people I ever met or saw, made you feel better, you know, warmed your heart.' Ashamed of my ignorance of the local traditions I eventually plucked up courage to tell him that I hadn't heard whom he was talking about. 'Oh,' he said, 'Marie Lloyd.' All this has made me wonder what it is that makes people happy. I asked myself what when I am happy makes me happy. What are the conditions which have produced happiness? I knew that gin didn't and that sex in itself didn't, I was pretty certain that success in itself didn't, because here the appetite grows on what it feeds on and one is always left asking for more, like gin and sex I suppose. I came eventually to the conclusion that there was only one source of lasting happiness, and that is the sense of belonging. To the degree in which we feel we belong, to that degree we're happy. To the degree in which we feel we don't belong, to that degree we feel unhappy. And often we try to assuage our unhappiness by malice, cruelty, bitching, because these things provide a substitute for belonging, rather like getting roaring drunk because your girl friend can't come for the weekend.

In our actual experience, of course, belonging is an ambiguous state of affairs. We belong to all sorts of groups; family, friends, race, class, school, college, faculty, and so on. And sometimes we're aware of their value and at other times we're aware only of their disadvantages. On me, as an earthly institution, the Church has this sort of double effect: there are times when I am proud and grateful to be a member of it and there are other times when I feel that being a member of the Church is like being in a spiritual gas chamber. (You can take that how you like.) But the apparent ambiguity is in fact an ambiguity about semantics not about the actual state of belonging. For when we dislike what we belong to and feel uncomfortable with it, all it means is that an important part of us doesn't belong—we

belong with one half and don't belong with the other. I
suppose none of us fully escapes this sort of ambivalence.
One of the chief ways it manifests is in our feelings towards
the people with whom we are connected in varying degrees
of intimacy. We are first aware of the half that belongs to
them, and then there emerges slowly or suddenly the half
that doesn't belong to them and we feel angry with them
and aggrieved. We're all caught up in this kind of ambivalence though it manifests in different ways in different people.
That's why Jesus was always stressing the need to forgive
others if we ourselves are to be forgiven. When somebody
manifests towards us the half that doesn't belong to us, a
similar non-belonging half in us is liable to be brought to
the surface and reinforced; and thus a vicious spiral begins
to grow. Only by willingness to receive the other person in
spite of the half in him or her which doesn't belong to us,
only so can we consolidate and build up in ourselves the
belonging half and diminish the non-belonging. Perhaps the
most reassuring thing about Christians is their willingness
to forgive. They should by profession be experts in forgiveness and such, in fact, they generally are. It shows that
belonging is more characteristic of them than not belonging
and that in turn shows that happiness is more characteristic
of them than its opposite.

But it's time we investigated this belonging of which so
far we have spoken a great deal without describing what it is.
The human societies to which we belong, family, friends,
country and so on, obviously don't take us to the heart of
the matter. For there is as we have seen in this kind of
belonging a degree of externality. We belong by external
circumstances to what we feel we don't fully belong to. The
sense of belonging may be greatly fostered and encouraged
by the human societies of which we're members and without human societies of some kind or other we couldn't feel
that we belonged at all. But it is as if these human societies
mediated something greater and other than themselves. They
are, if you like, the soil, the sun and the rain by means of
which alone the plant can grow, but the biological life of
the plant—what makes it grow—is something different. And
this is particularly manifest when, in some uncongenial soil
where there is too little sun or too little rain, you see a
plant pushing itself up as though determined to exist in

spite of its environment. So people with unhappy back-grounds can grow in their sense of belonging.

But what then is the essence of belonging? It's the aware-ness that as a living being I am an organic part of a greater whole and the knowledge that nothing whatever can separate me from that greater whole. This fundamental fact of human existence has been expressed in a variety of ways in a variety of religions and philosophies. Its most recent full expres-sion can be found in the works of C. G. Jung. Few people in the modern world have been more aware than Jung that in the inner realm of the psyche the individual person is part and parcel of influences and forces which are infinite in number and too mysterious to be scientifically analysed and catalogued. He believed that these forces were creative, that we owed to them every valuable achievement, and that they were destructive only when blindly resisted. And when he spoke of the conscious mind being open to receive what the unconscious had to say, he was asking the individual to become aware that he was inalienably part of a comprehen-sive totality, whoever he was and whatever his external cir-cumstances.

It's easy enough to laugh at Jung (as it's easy enough to laugh at the New Testament) but I expect we've all in fact put Jung to the test and found him true. Why is it, for instance, that *Antigone* or *King Lear* or the *Brothers Kara-mazov* seem to be describing ourselves? Isn't it because Sophocles and Shakespeare and Dostoevsky were subject to the same influences and belong to the same totality as we do? Or, what again, in art or music, is the attraction of the primitive? Isn't it that it reminds us of areas to which we inherently belong but which we've often forgotten or ignored? Jung arrived at his conclusions by his own observa-tion and thought, but that by nature we belong to every-thing and that therefore everything belongs to us has been a central tenet of Christian conviction since the start. We live, therefore we belong.

Whatever the language or idiom used to describe this truth, it is of so profound and mysterious a nature that it can't be set out with the kind of intellectual precision with which more superficial things can be described. And here I must remind you of something insisted upon by the father of philosophy, that there are realities too real to be described

directly and which therefore have to be described indirectly
by what he called myth. But myth, we need hardly be
reminded, doesn't mean fable but truth too true for abstract
concepts. And that at least is one thing that Plato and Jesus
have in common—they both used myths or parables when
speaking of what was almost too true for words.

Of such a kind, Christians would claim, is the truth of
Christ. Christ is the totality in whose being everything is
gathered together and revealed as one. When Christian
orthodoxy affirms that in Christ you find perfect Godhead
and perfect manhood united in one person what at least it
is saying is that there is no life or experience or power or
reality of any kind whatever that is excluded from his identity. Whatever is, is part of Christ.

That may seem strange when you think of the negative and
destructive forces by which we are surrounded. How can
hatred, cruelty, despair and so on be part of Christ and
included in his identity? But the New Testament, in strange
and straining language, speaks of Christ becoming sin for
us. It speaks of him taking the form of a slave, subjecting
himself to Adam's curse, agonising so that his sweat was as it
were great drops of blood falling upon the ground, suffering
in a violent death the final onslaught of destructive evil.

Evil is the perversion of life. Destructiveness, for instance,
is the perversion of creativity. It's those who have evaded
the challenge to create who set out as a substitute to destroy.
The raw material of hatred is the capacity to love. Love plus
rejection which means love plus pain generally equals hatred.
The language of the New Testament suggests that Christ, by
being willing to receive and to take upon himself as his own
all the perversions of life, changed their character, straightened
out their crookedness, made them once again the raw material
of goodness. Of this the visual representation is the central
Christian symbol of the cross. That gallows on which an
utterly good man was murdered at the age of thirty-three is
the place where we feel most loved, most accepted, most
capable of ourselves doing good. Hence one of the earliest
Christian hymns speaks of sweetest wood and sweetest iron
while the New Testament speaks of Christ's death as a
ransom as though the potentiality for good which is everywhere had been brought back from the perversions to which
it was enslaved. And Christian faith sees everything in the

light of that ransom. When, for instance, Dr. Martin Luther King was shot dead, Christ was present not only in the heroism of the assassinated leader but also in the hatred and violence of the assassin, for it was that very hatred and violence that Christ took upon himself at Calvary, unravelling its hideous knots and using it to show what love means.

So the point still stands: whatever is, is part of Christ. Just as a person's physical body is both the vehicle of his presence and in some way or other identified with him, so everything in heaven and on earth is the vehicle of Christ's presence and in some way or other identified with him. The birth of a child, the lilies of the field, Solomon in all his glory, the infinite expanses of outer space, the violence of a mob, the assassin's bullet, the sweet warmth of friendship, the tortured man's despair, the tenderness of human love and the cruelty of human hatred: in all these places Christ is present, they are the vehicle of his real presence, preserving, rescuing, unravelling, healing, converting, transforming. There is no place of any kind whatsoever within us or outside where the Redeemer is not redeeming and where the Saviour is not saving. Bishop Westcott once said that in St. John's Gospel the story of the Passion is set out as a revelation of majesty. That revelation of majesty is present with us at all times and in all places whatever happens. That is Christ's achievement, that he has gathered everything to himself both of good and of evil so that in all, had we but the eyes to see him, we might behold the fair beauty of the Lord. Perhaps therefore the only prayer we need ever pray is that of the blind beggar, 'Lord Jesus, that I may receive my sight.'

There is, you see, in the most literal sense no such thing as a lonely soul, only a soul which is blind to the indissoluble ties which unite it with everything that is. Sometimes we're aware of how we thus belong. Confronted, shall we say, with some great scene of natural beauty we're moved to what is in fact the form of contemplation. The mountains or the meadows that we see aren't felt as something alien to us which shuts us out. We feel deeply if inarticulately that we belong, that what we see is an element of our own identity. It's not for nothing that the Bible tells us that the Lord God formed man out of the dust of the ground. This same sense of belonging is true of our work when it goes well. To the scientist or scholar his laboratory or library is not an alien land. He feels truly part of his work, and he's happy because he knows that he belongs to what he does. Christians would describe these experiences as the presence of Christ who, in St. Paul's words, fills all things.

But of course it's with other people that most of us are chiefly concerned and it's communion with other people that most of us want more than anything else. And this desire for communion includes as an inevitable part of it a very deep-seated wish to be of service to others, to help them, to be of use. It's true that this can be used to minister to our own egotism when we want to pose to ourselves and others as saviour figures. I believe in the reality of what some psychiatrists describe as a Christ complex. But the perversion of something good doesn't destroy the reality of its goodness. Helping people often obviously calls for action. But however essential it may often be to take action on behalf of others, it's not, I firmly believe, by action that we help them most. For the outward contact we have with people is no more than the external visible sign of an inward unseen communion. We can help people most by living for them as Jesus did, offering ourselves to God on their behalf in all we are and do. So the night before he died Jesus prayed for his friends and said, 'For their sake I now dedicate myself that they too may be dedicated in truth.' If in the silence of our own prayer we sincerely give ourselves to God on behalf of other people, then we can leave specific actions to look after themselves. We'll do them all right and what's more we shall prevent ourselves doing more harm than good. In any case, people in the deepest need are in the last resort unapproachable on the level of external contact. But just as Jesus accepted his approaching death, we can accept some handicap or disappointment or frustration or duty that has come our way, and pray to God of his loving kindness to use it to bring help to the afflicted or joy to those we love, or peace on earth. The truth of our inter-connection has been well described by the French writer Léon Bloy in his own poetic idiom:

'An impulse of real pity sings the praises of God from the time of Adam to the end of the world. It cures the sick, consoles those in despair, calms the raging of the

sea, ransoms those in prison, recovers the lost and protects mankind.'

But as members one of another in Christ we're not only
donors. We're much more recipients. When, after a period
of darkness, light floods into our hearts, when some load is
shed, when we have been enabled to do the right thing, when
if you like we recover a lost sense of belonging, isn't all that
because we do in fact belong, with the result that spiritual
and moral victories achieved by others have come to our
rescue and stood us on our feet? 'No one lives and no one
dies for himself alone,' says St. Paul. This deep interpene-
tration of all souls with each other is in the Christian vocabu-
lary called the communion of saints. That phrase doesn't
refer to a huddle of pious people. It means that we're all
one in Christ, that in Christ we belong intimately to each
other, that there is a continuous and mutual traffic between us
all, that as an individual person I belong to everybody who
has ever lived and that they belong to me.

To our ordinary way of thinking that may sound fantastic.
But our mind is a limited instrument and it's only common
sense that we can't empty the ocean into a bucket.

In so far as in our inmost being we grasp the truth that in
Christ all things are ours, whether this person or that person or the other person or the world or life or death or
things present or things to come, in so far as we grasp that
all things are ours, we shall be happy with a happiness of
which literally nothing can rob us.

ARTS, SCIENCES AND LAW

CHAPTER TEN

THE CREATIVE SPIRIT

by C. DAY LEWIS, Esq.,
Poet Laureate

'Art is a house which tries to be haunted.' These words, written by Emily Dickinson in a letter to a friend, go straight to the heart of the mystery of the creative spirit. Every art is both an art and a craft. In painting, in music, in poetry, the practitioner is committed to a lifelong struggle with his medium: but he knows that all this devotion, all this perseverance cannot guarantee success—they can only make it possible—make it possible for the mysterious X to enter into a work and inhabit there.

X, the unknown quantity, has been called inspiration. Plato believed that poets are possessed by a god. The Neo-Platonists insisted that it is not phenomenal nature which true poets imitated, but the archetypal reality behind nature. Coleridge defined genius as 'possessing the spirit, not possessed by it'. There is clearly a radical change of ground here. But a common factor is found in all such definitions of the source of art: that common factor is, spirit. The poet knows that this spirit is a wind which bloweth where it listeth. He cannot command its presence. If he is lucky, it may whisk him aloft for a few years, or a few weeks: then it drops him, it may be for ever. But he is aware that, perhaps only once or twice in a lifetime, he has written beyond the capacity of his craft. How has this happened?

The Greeks called memory 'the mother of the Muses'. For the artist, memory seems to work in a specialised way. It depends, paradoxically, on forgetfulness. Robert Frost spoke about 'the surprise of remembering something I didn't know I knew'. What seems to happen for a poet is that experience sinks down on to the seabed of the unconscious. And lying there for a length of time, it is changed: 'those are pearls that were his eyes'. And one day a fragment of this buried treasure floats to the surface. It comes to me, very often, in an enigmatic form—a form of words, a brief phrase, which is attended by a special feeling of anticipation, excitement. It comes, more often than not, quite unexpectedly, when the mind is in neutral, or thinking of something else. I recognise in it the seed of a poem. It is, in fact, both a seed and a signpost; for it contains within it the potency of the still unwritten poem, and it points the direction this poem should take. I meditate on this *donnée*, this riddling clue, seeking to pick out, from the many possible meanings it suggests, the right meaning—the one which should grow into the theme of the poem.

From now on, everything has to be worked for: the craft takes over. But the *donnée* is for free. Of course, one usually misinterprets it, or botches it in the process of constructing the poem. But this initial *donnée*—if it is the real article and not a plausible substitute—comes surely as a kind of grace; grace which cannot be commanded, expected or even deserved.

I could not possibly dismiss the belief that what is given to the artist from time to time is a form of *divine* grace. It may be convenient nowadays to speak in terms of individual psychology, or of a collective unconscious which the poet can tap to make his myths of 'archetypal reality'. But such explanations do not fully satisfy: they do not explain the poet's conviction that, perhaps once or twice only in his life, he has come close to the Ground of Being.

Fortunately for him, he does not have to justify this conviction. His business is to write poems, not to theorise about their source. And the artist is indeed a singularly fortunate man. He is fortunate in his vocation—in being a person wide open to the creative spirit. He is fortunate because, on however infinitesimal a scale, he is doing the work of creation; brooding over a chaos of formless energy—memories, thoughts, feelings, images—and making a pattern of it, reducing it to order. He recognises himself as a man under authority—like Robert Browning's poet:

Through a whole campaign of the world's life and death
Doing the King's work all the dim day long.

But, if he differs from other men, it is in degree, not in kind. The instinct to make something, to make something

grow—a table, a baby, a garden trellis or a scientific hypothesis—we know to be universal. However humble or exalted
the thing made, however ephemeral or long-lived, it has come
into being through the operation of the creative spirit. It is
possible, and right, to take pride in what is a work of many
hands—a controlled experiment, a ship, an aircraft. From
such working units, the artist differs because his work is
solitary: because it is solitary, it can tempt him to satanic
egotism; because his ideal is perfection, he is often in danger
of falling into despair. If he avoids these dangers, it is
because the spirit which commands him to create also
demands that he shall communicate. The man who calls his
wife into the workshop and says, 'Look what I've made,' is
following the same impulse as the poet who hands a friend
a finished poem and asks, 'Have I made something of it?'

What is it that the poet wishes to communicate? An
experience, a state of mind, a moral truth, a spiritual explora-
tion. It may be any of these; it is often all of them. He tries
to understand experience by re-creating it in terms of his
art, to make sense of it *for himself*. If he succeeds, something will be communicated to his readers: he does not start
off with the need to convey it to others—communication is
the seal, but as it were a by-product, of his struggle with
words. Every artist must strive to approach as near as he can
to the core or essence of Being, and force it to reveal a little
of its secret:

> *Myself must I remake*
> *Till I am Timon and Lear*
> *Or that William Blake*
> *Who beat upon the wall*
> *Till Truth obeyed his call.*

I find it difficult to imagine that any artist, who is not a
mere doodler with words, notes or paint, can be a materialist.
The sources of his art are so deep: though it must use space
and time, the art springs from a region where time and space
are unimportant.

I would like to end with a few words about the human
qualities which are required if the workings of the creative
spirit are to go forward unimpeded. They are, I believe,
three—patience, joy, disinterestedness. The artist's calling

demands that he be disinterested, should have no axe to grind, should rid himself as far as possible of the notion of his art as a way of self-advancement (if he is a poet, he soon learns it will not make him large sums of money). But disinterestedness goes further. It involves a detachment from personal concerns as well as from ambition. However private, intimate, urgent may have been the experience which gives rise to a poem, when the poem is finished, if it is a good poem, it is much more than a piece of 'self-expression'. It is out there, a part of the Other: the poet has made it, and in the course of making it, has withdrawn himself, distanced himself, from it. Had he not done so, the poem's power to communicate, to say something meaningful to others, would have been fatally impaired.

Joy is essential; the joy the artist takes in his work, its technical rigours and rewards. That certainly. But also the joy which is an affirmation of life. 'These poems,' said Dylan Thomas of his own collected work, 'with all their crudities, doubts, and confusions, are written for the love of Man and in praise of God.' The passionate interest an artist takes in the world around him and the world in his head—not only its beauty, challenge and amenity but equally its squalors and tragedies—and his compulsion to praise them by responding to them and in some sort reproducing them—this interest and compulsion are the gifts of the creative spirit.

In the exercise of his art, patience is paramount. Patience to accumulate his memories, to let them bide till they are ready; patience in wrestling with a shadowy intimation and forcing it to yield up its truth—wrestling with the angel patience to sustain him through many failures, through many dark nights and false dawns. But above all, in the words of Rilke, 'it is the memories themselves that matter. Only when they have turned to blood within us, to glance and gesture, nameless and no longer to be distinguished from ourselves —only then can it happen that in a most rare hour the first word of a poem arises in their midst and goes forth from them.'

'Art is a house which tries to be haunted.' I was attempting to interpret and enlarge upon this in a poem called *Final Instructions*. This poem uses the figure of an old pagan priest, the head of a college of priests, sending out a pupil to begin his ministry. It is a poem about vocation and especially about the kind of grace which the creative artist must hope but cannot expect to receive. Specifically, the god in the poem is the Muse: but I would like to think that the poem has meaning for every man and woman, no matter what his profession, who has a sense of vocation and a hope of grace, who is prepared to lay himself on the altar and offer again and again what he has to offer.

Final Instructions

For sacrifice, there are certain principles—
Few, but essential.

I do not mean your ritual. This you have learnt—
The garland, the salt, a correct use of the knife,
And what to do with the blood;
Though it is worth reminding you that no two
Sacrifices ever turn out alike—
Not where this god is concerned.

The celebrant's approach may be summed up
In three words—patience, joy,
Disinterestedness. Remember, you do not sacrifice
For your own glory or peace of mind:
You are there to assist the clients and please the god.

It goes without saying
That only the best is good enough for the god.
But the best—I must emphasise it—even your best
Will by no means always be found acceptable.
Do not be discouraged:
Some lizard or passing cats may taste your sacrifice
And bless the god: it will not be entirely wasted.

But the crucial point is this:
You are called only to make the sacrifice:
Whether or no he enters into it
Is the god's affair; and whatever the handbooks say,
You can neither command his presence nor explain it—
All you can do is to make it possible.
If the sacrifice catches fire of its own accord

On the altar, well and good. But do not
Flatter yourself that discipline and devotion
Have wrought the miracle: they have only allowed it.

So luck is all I can wish you, or need wish you.
And every time you prepare to lay yourself
On the altar and offer again what you have to offer,
Remember, my son,
Those words—patience, joy, disinterestedness.

CHAPTER ELEVEN

CHRIST AND PASSION MUSIC

by SIR THOMAS ARMSTRONG,
formerly Principal, the Royal Academy of Music

(Before this address the men of King's College Choir sang part of Vittoria's setting of the Passion according to St. John.)

The Passion that you have just heard is one of the finest of the pre-Reformation settings, but may have been a surprise to those who associate passion music primarily with Bach. It's understandable that many people's thoughts should turn first to Bach in this connection, since it was his genius that produced, as culmination of a growth that had extended over many centuries, a masterpiece that has eclipsed other settings, some smaller in size, like Vittoria's, but not less perfect in their own way.

It's a pity that in admiring great masterpieces we are apt to overlook the smaller ones, or to deny them the attention that would reveal their quality; and this has very often happened in music and in connection with passion music. And if we associate the St. Matthew Passion primarily with a Lutheran composer, it's because Bach, in providing a Good Friday Three Hours' Devotion for St. Thomas Church in Leipzig, produced a work so masterly that it has spread far beyond the purposes for which it was primarily intended, and been acclaimed by many to whom the circumstances in which it was originally planned would have been alien and perhaps distasteful. When we speak of a Lutheran master we at once admit that the intentions and circumstances of this particular work, despite its grandeur, were limited. And it's true, moreover, that a large part of the history of passion music lies far behind any influence of Luther or of Bach, in those centuries of earlier devotion that produced so many of the greatest masterpieces of European art. Nor could passion music even be said to be a purely European achievement, since there were many diverse tributaries that emptied themselves into the great stream of pre-Reformation liturgical music, and into the plainsong which forms such an important part of that tradition. It's almost certain, for instance, that Byzantine influences were at work in the early chant, and that these influences connect catholic liturgical music with important sources outside Europe.

The musico-dramatic treatment of the Passion Story sprang from a desire to make more vivid the narrative that was recited year by year in the Passiontide offices: it belongs especially to the life of those religious orders that were attempting to focus upon the events of Holy Week and Easter the undivided attention of a single-minded community. These liturgies, influenced by the requirements of conventual Churches, included the Passion Story within the general plan of the whole Holy Week cycle. This great effort, which may claim to stand as one of the most complete achievements of European art—comparable with the greatest cathedrals or pictures, comparable with the Ring and other works of the finest quality—this great effort began on Palm Sunday when the first of the passions was recited, passed through the whole week to the Good Friday passion according to St. John which you have just heard, and finally reached the triumph of the Gospel in the High Mass on Easter Day. In each case where it was included, the narrative of the passion formed only a part of the liturgy; and its musical setting remained an episode, an important episode but not the principal event of the cycle. Each service of devotion, from Palm Sunday to Easter, though complete in itself, was also part of a whole week's pattern, like one scene in an opera and in the different operas of a cycle. The influence of this fact is far-reaching, since the musical treatment of the narratives, so long as it formed a part of the Mass, could not be allowed to spread itself beyond reasonable limits. Even in the later settings, like the one you have just heard, when crowd choruses were becoming more elaborate, these remained compact, and were not permitted to develop into extended movements.

This very concentration, forced upon the form by its limitations and its purpose, is a powerful element, since the focusing of the whole attention on a limited area can produce an intensity of vision which is not possible in a wider field. It's like the music of the clavichord, so soft as to be inaudible if one is only a few yards away, yet holding within its narrow compass, once the ear is adjusted to its scale, a whole world of musical experience. This is a great mystery, one of the many mysteries of music: a single note, a solitary voice, can mean as much as a symphony. And when the narrator in a plainsong passion recites within the strict limits of that conventual chant (in the St. Matthew Passion, for instance, when Peter went out into the darkness and cold and wept bitterly), the effect of the chant can be every bit as moving as Bach's tortured *melisma*, and even more moving, because more is left to the audience. Bach's elaboration, marvellous in itself, can constitute a check upon the imagination of an individual listener.

In the ceremonies of the Lutheran Tomaskirche, passion music occupied a different place—a more important place, but a more isolated one. Instead of constituting one element among many in the Mass and in the whole procession of Passion Week ceremonies, the passion became a particular meditation like the Three Hours' Service, more or less dramatic in character, associated with a long sermon; those undertones which had been so significant, although private, in the Catholic passions, became explicit and public. Influences began to creep in from opera and from oratorio; and once the incidents of the passion were allowed to become the subjects of meditative poems written by the clergy, the floodgates were open to all the eccentricities of emotional, pietistic literary effort. The reasons for this were deep-seated in the character of the north German people, as well as among the influences of that terrible Thirty Years' War, which had left in every family its legends of suffering, disaster and death. For such a people, at such a time, insistence upon the details of torture and suffering was natural enough; and upon these some of their Good Friday meditations tended to concentrate. It would be sadly true to say that torture and suffering are common enough in the modern world, and so constantly before our eyes as to form to some extent a daily experience for those who are capable of sympathy. And yet, it remains true that the vivid imagery of revivalist preaching, whether in Lutheran poems or Methodist hymns, can hardly be acceptable on a wide basis unless the work in which they are concerned is lifted to a high level by the genius of a master. This is what happened in the case of Bach; but even in the settings by Bach there are moments when the influence of soliloquy or theological comment seems to detract from the power which is exerted by a plain recitation of the story, without comment, such as you heard in the passion by Vittoria.

From the point we've reached, with the development of music in Europe and the decline of ecclesiastical influence, the Passion Story began to overflow from purely Christian worship into the musical interpretation of human experience as a whole. Wagner came to a point when he was forced to attempt some synthesis of Christian mysticism with his own romantic mythology. But the symbolism of *Parsifal* is very hard to understand; and the attempt to reproduce in a pagan world the ceremonies of the Mass itself has proved distasteful to many people, including some who admire Wagner. The meaning in *Parsifal* becomes clear only when music begins to exercise undisputed sway, and reveals the underlying truths that Wagner found it difficult to explain in words or symbolism. Music alone is only able to convey these truths because it is not necessary for music to particularise it in words that are capable of misunderstanding. In more recent times Britten's *War Requiem* has drawn together the Catholic liturgy and the poetry of present-day sacrifice, but with results that are not completely satisfying. There are some who question not the sincerity or mastery of Britten's invention but the suitability of equating the voluntary sacrifice of the sinless being whom many have regarded as the only begotten Son of God with the great but different sacrifice of a conscript soldier. Of course it's true that the sacrifice of Christ is a type and an honoured summary of all sacrifice; it's true that there have been in the past countless crucifixions among all classes of people, and that daily sacrifices which might be called crucifixions are taking place within the experience of us all. Moreover, frequent sacrificial deaths have been extorted by society or by individuals, deaths like those of Socrates and Galileo, of Joan of Arc, of Thomas More, of Anne Frank, of those nuns and missionaries in the Congo, of that teacher who willingly offered her own death to save the lives of her pupils. Yet there still remains some difference, because we cannot be sure how far these sacrifices were a voluntary oblation and satisfaction, nor do we believe that the victims were the only begotten

Son of God, although in many, many cases, if we had been standing by among the onlookers, we might have echoed the words of the centurion, that non-Christian observer who said, 'Truly this was the Son of God.'

If we are seeking words of Christ himself which might be applicable to the attempts of musicians to interpret the Passion Story, I suppose we should think first of the injunction, 'This do in remembrance of me', an injunction which was repeated by the Apostle and amplified with the words, 'Do all in the name of Christ.' But the teachings and example of Christ are so all-pervading and so general in their application that one hardly needs to select, or to particularise: the man who is working in the spirit of Christ in music or in any other art will find in every crisis and every problem the guidance that he needs but may not be ready to accept. Many indeed are the words that seem especially adapted to our attempt to perform passion music. We have to ask ourselves what is our basic motive in doing this at all: why should we be trying to devote our effort and energy to the task of securing a good performance? A musician could, I suppose, make this complete offering of his talents and, perhaps, of himself, from various motives. He might do it to enhance his professional reputation; he might do it to earn his living; he could do it as a tribute to a great composer, or a tribute to music itself. Or, having agreed to participate as a professional duty, he could offer his best endeavour because of some sense of professional obligation, some sense of loyalty to tradition, and to his own craftsmanship. And these loyalties are not to be underrated, since their roots lie in the soil where religion itself takes nourishment. But they are different from the motives that animate a Christian who is doing his work, within whatever field it may lie, in remembrance of Christ. And the results that should follow from a self-dedication of this kind are far-reaching, since they affect not only the artist himself but also his attitude to all those who are associated with him in the act of remembrance, whether as performers or as audience.

It is here perhaps that we come close to the heart of the matter. The Passion Story itself, and one's musical response to it, constitute a direct challenge to every person, in each episode of the narration, and in every aspect of life. It affects us as human beings, it affects us as musicians, it affects us deeply if we are trying to be Christians. And perhaps among these many impacts the most forcible of all is its rebuke to pride, to our pride in technical skill, in our impeccable taste, and in the very traditions of craftsmanship that make our work possible. That sense of pride in caste and professional tradition goes far to explain the attitudes of the high priest and his colleagues. But if we are inclined to condemn the high priest we must also judge ourselves; and ask whether there is any direct commendation at all by Christ for those who participated in these events. No direct commendation, I think, for those who might perhaps have expected or hoped to receive it; for the Apostles it was, 'Why trouble ye the women?', or 'Could ye not watch with me one hour?' For the soldiers it was 'Are ye come against me as against a thief with swords and staves for to take me?' And in the settings of the passion music, both those of Bach and those of the pre-Reformation composers, there is no cadence more tragic than that which sets the words, 'Then all the disciples forsook him and fled.' And yet there are commendations, perhaps for two persons in the Passion Story. The first is the thief on the cross; the second the woman who had been so recently rebuked by the self-righteous. 'She did it for my burial,' Christ had said; and when we think upon this episode we find it hard to forget the opening line with which the poet began: 'She was a harlot and he was a thief.' But I suppose she was commended because she had done her best at personal cost to herself only for love; and this word of Christ may help us more than any other to understand our responsibilities in the performance of passion music and may provide us with the best motive for what we are trying to do; perhaps the only one, and it may also save us from the danger of belittling or making fun of the efforts of others who choose to commemorate the passion in ways that are different from our own, by means of music that does not happen to suit our particular taste, although it may have been helpful to more of our fellow-Christians than have ever had a chance to hear a Bach passion.

Sometimes during a rehearsal or a concert an artist will stop and ask himself how the composer would react if he were suddenly to walk into the room. 'What would Bach say if he heard us trying to rehearse this chorus? What would Beethoven say if he came in and found us singing the Missa

Solemnis?' We know from comments actually made on some occasions what Beethoven himself might have said, but we have to go further than this, and ask what Christ would say if he were to attend one of our performances of the St. Matthew Passion—perhaps in the Royal Festival Hall or in some cathedral or college chapel—or if he were to go into a village church or chapel where they were singing Stainer's *Crucifixion* or Maunder's *From Olivet to Calvary*. Would he find fault with the sentiment and style of these works? Or would he, if he were in the Royal Festival Hall, scourge us all out and overthrow the tables of the money-changers, as we went to the treasurer's office to collect our fees? 'My house shall be called the house of prayer for all nations and ye have made it a den of thieves.' This is a hard saying; one of many. Would he say, 'Woe unto you hypo-crites for ye built the sepulchres of the prophets and garnish the tombs of the righteous, and behold I send unto you wise men and prophets and scribes, some of them ye kill and scourge and some of them you crucify in your synagogues and persecute from city to city, that upon you may come all the righteous blood that is shed upon the earth?' What a terrible indictment! How humbling to have to accept these words, 'Upon us, upon us, all the righteous blood that is shed upon the earth.' But perhaps he would admonish us with gentler warnings: perhaps he would say, 'Whensoever you stand praying, forgive if ye have aught against anyone.' Or would he repeat once more those words that are recorded by St. Luke at the very end of his Gospel, 'Ye are witnesses of these things and behold I send forth the promise of my Father, but tarry ye in the city until ye be clothed with power from on high'? Every phrase of the sentence is preg-nant with meaning for the artist. 'Tarry ye in the city'—no escapism—'tarry ye in the city'; 'clothed with power'. Ah! If only it could be so, if you and I could only be clothed with power! But power for what? Not power to win the world, not power for any of the purposes for which people usually desire it. Christ went on to specify: 'Power that repentance and remission of sins should be preached in his name unto all the nations.' Those are the words of Christ, 'power for the remission of sins'. And so we are left here saying for our-selves the words, 'God be merciful to me the sinner.'

As we go back into the Passion Story, and the Gospels

themselves, to seek out those utterances of Christ's that apply especially to passion music, more immediately if one is contemplating a performance, we are faced with the terrifying rebukes that are reserved for self-righteousness, callousness, hypocrisy and pride. These are the disqualifying disabilities; from them, for the artist, or anyone who is trying to live as an artist, spring arrogance, self-absorption, excessive ambition, cupidity, and bad taste. These are dangers in any professional career, but especially an artistic one; and we become more than ever conscious, with increasing experience, of the influence of these defects of character upon artistic achievement. It is, in fact, scarcely too much to say that all artistic failures, all exploitations, all lapses into bad taste, are moral failures. And yet at the same time one becomes newly aware, forcibly aware and refreshingly aware, of the unfailing recognition that was accorded by Christ to the virtues of simplicity, humility and the power of love. 'Except ye become as little children', he seems constantly to be saying; and in many utterances where these words are not specifically mentioned they seem to reverberate. 'Whosoever shall not receive the kingdom as a little child he shall in no wise enter therein.' And through all the variations of the Gospel story there echoes the promise that is like a recurring and tender cadence in music: 'Where two or three are gathered together in my name, there am I in the midst of them';—'in my name', 'two or three'. In such simple words the problem is stated, and the solution indicated, if we could understand rightly. But the attempt to understand leads us deep into an examination of our motives, ourselves, and the nature of the effort that we are making, whether in a performance of the St. Matthew Passion or in any other artistic endeavour.

CHAPTER TWELVE

RELIGION AND SCIENCE

by Professor W. H. THORPE, F.R.S., Department of
Animal Behaviour, Cambridge University

I have a vivid memory of an occasion in my first under-
graduate year. A friend, also a freshman, suggested we should
go to hear some distinguished speaker, whose name I have
long forgotten, on the theme 'Science and Religion'. I dis-
suaded him by saying, 'Surely no one can have anything
new to say today on such an overworked and wellworn topic.'
It strikes me as distinctly comic that I should now be standing in this pulpit addressing you on the self-same subject.
And I wonder how many have stayed away tonight for the
same reason that I gave forty-five years ago!

But why was I so wrong? What makes the subject peren-
nial? There are, I think, various answers to that question.
For instance, one answer is that the power and penetration
of the scientific method have proved far greater and more
pervasive than most people then suspected. But this answer
is itself, in part, an outcome of the immense avalanche of
scientific activity that we have witnessed. To show that this
really is an avalanche, let me remind you that a perfectly
sober calculation suggests that of all the scientists who have
ever lived, ninety per cent are alive today! To put it differ-
ently: the average annual world population growth is two
per cent; that of scientists is six per cent!

Before going further I must, to avoid confusion, explain
what I mean this evening by the two words in my title.
What do we mean by 'science'? Strictly this means all knowledge. By popular usage it has become more or less restricted
to knowledge about objects in the natural world, to 'natural
science'. Two other characteristics are worth pointing out.
Most working scientists, if they are not too much bothered
by philosophy, adhere to the practical working hypothesis
that all natural events have a natural cause. The second
characteristic is very fundamental to our topic: it is clear

that the structure of human scientific knowledge about the world is never, and can never be, complete. There is always the possibility that some fundamental discovery may be made which will require modification of at least large parts of it. Scientific authority can never therefore be absolutely secure. It is open to anyone to upset it all if he can. Indeed, it is part of the spirit of science that he should try his best to do so. Freedom is therefore secure. But the greater part of scientific knowledge is sufficiently established to have a certain authority. Thus, as Dr. Joseph Needham pointed out many years ago, science provides the most perfect resolution which man has yet found of the antinomy between authority and freedom.

Now as to religion. Religion means the belief that interpenetrating the natural environment perceived by our senses, there exists beyond it a larger environment without which the visible environment cannot be full comprehended, and to which men must relate themselves. This is what Tillich calls 'the ultimate concern which is manifest in all creative functions of the human spirit'. But having adopted this extremely general definition of religion can we find a similarly general definition of the Christian religion? I suggest that we can; and say, 'Christianity is the belief in the fatherhood of God and the brotherhood of Man as primarily set forth in the life and teachings of Jesus.' You will at once see from these definitions that religion is essentially 'mystical' in the real sense of that much abused word, namely, that mysticism is concerned with the awareness of values, in part at least, above and beyond the scope of current symbolism to express; in particular the intense awareness of the whole as the unity of all things. In short it comes near the idea of the 'holy'. Mystical Christianity is thus a spiritual religion based on a firm belief in absolute and eternal values as the most real things in the universe, and a confidence that these values are knowable by man. It follows that this knowledge, which is of all things most precious, can only be approached by a whole-hearted consecration of the intellect, will and affections of man. And this is a faith which all men need.

We shall consider in a moment how far, if at all, this mysticism is alien to the nature and methods of science.

Wherein then lies any conflict there may be between the scientific and the religious outlook? I believe it lies primarily in the ideas of 'reductionism' or 'nothing buttery' as it is sometimes called; the idea, for example, that an organism is 'nothing but' the atoms, electrons and molecules of which its body is composed.

There is no doubt that society today, accustomed to the alluring vistas of new and ever expanding knowledge of the world and the seemingly endless developments in the technological mastery over nature, is far more receptive of rationalist–mechanist philosophies than others, simply because it considers such views as more 'scientific' than other alternatives. Much of society's acceptance of this is in fact based on a misunderstanding of science itself. I believe it is vital that some of these widespread misconceptions, regarded by many as self-evident, should be countered and corrected.

Everyone knows that science involves the construction of theories, conceived to some degree at least in mechanistic terms—theories which are then tested experimentally to see whether they stand up to practical laboratory investigation. But there is a widespread tendency among ordinary people, and indeed among scientists, to assume that the scientific view of the world as an interlocking series of mechanisms can be the basis of a general philosophy. Scientists make such assumptions as practical working hypotheses for everyday use; deliberately, for practical purposes, leaving out of the picture the mind, the perception and the personal devotion of the scientist making the study. This approach, when extended to the whole of experience, can be called 'mechanistic monism'.

The average non-scientist, therefore, thinks of science as being concerned mainly, if not exclusively, with what in fact is simply the experimental or analytical part; that part which, in the laboratory, certainly occupies most working scientists for most of their time, but which is ultimately sterile without the constructive, imaginative, creative insight which is the basis for most of the major developments in science—whether physical or biological.

If we look through the list of recent Nobel prize-winners it becomes obvious that many, perhaps a large majority, achieve this reward by something very different; by great leaps of imaginative insight; leaps which, at the time at which they were made, may have had very little experimental or observational basis. (Dirac, Niels Bohr, Watson and

Crick, Krebs, Bragg, Rutherford, Morgan, Eccles, Einstein, Hopkins among others, and going back to a much earlier generation—Mendel.) Discoveries of this type at their inception are often far removed from the work of the laboratory. Yet they played their role as great scientific theories because, though imaginative constructions of wide generality, they were also close enough to physical or biological reality to allow of experimental verification.

In 1877 Clerk Maxwell said, 'The name of physical science is often applied in a more or less restricted manner to those branches of science in which the phenomena considered are of the simplest and most abstract kind, excluding the consideration of the more complex phenomena, such as those observed in living beings.' This is the reason why physics and chemistry were the first sciences to become 'exact' and 'mature'—just because so much of the wealth of natural phenomena is excluded from their study. This selection or restriction enables them to make rapid progress with the help of mathematical models of high intellectual quality. As Carl Pantin once said, 'Very clever men are answering the relatively easy questions of the natural examination paper. Intellectually magnificent though the attack upon these problems has been, the problems they present are easier than those of the unrestricted sciences of which biology is the obvious example.' The physicist can restrict himself to physical problems and physico-mathematical concepts. The biologist may have to traverse many other sciences besides his own in order to arrive at a plausible explanation of the phenomena he is studying.

This primacy of the physical sciences can easily lead to what may be called the 'analytical fallacy': that understanding of a phenomenon is only to be gained by a study of the rules governing its component part. Although, as we shall see, it doesn't really apply even in physics. Thus we often seem to see a progressive analysis, starting with gross physical objects, the understanding of which depends on molecular analysis by the chemist, which in turn depends on knowledge of isotopes, which in turn depends upon the ever increasing array of ultimate particles handed down to us from on high by the nuclear physicist. To quote Pantin again, 'From here it is easy to pass to the fallacy that once we have found the correct assumptions necessary for the description of the ultimate particles, we have only to work out the consequences of these, together with the theory of probability, to describe the properties of all material configurations of more complex orders.' Thus we pass to the not uncommon view (not I may say held by the really informed men of science) that the world we perceive is an illusion and only the 'scientific' world of protons and electrons is real. This is nonsense because it is based on a gross fallacy and would destroy the very premises upon which science itself depends. For our 'knowledge' of protons and electrons is in fact based in the last resort upon the same senses and sense organs, the same powers of perception and abstraction, of synthesis, of symbol formation, of correlation, insight and classification as is our whole picture of the external world and of our own bodily and mental organisation. There is no justification whatever for accepting the reality of the one and denying that of the other.

In biology we see the same fallacy lurking. With the coming of Heisenberg, physics long ago departed from a naïve mechanistic picture of the outer world as made up of bundles of micro-precisely programmed chain-reactions. Rather the picture now is of organic entities as systems, subject to 'network-dynamics' and 'feedback'. While the major aspect of state and pattern of such systems can be unequivocally described as known, the detailed states and pathways of the components are so erratic as to defy definition; and even if some super Laplacean intelligence could trace them, they would be so unique and non-recurrent that they would be devoid of scientific interest. In fact Eddington put the problem simply and dramatically many years ago: 'We often think that when we have completed our study of "one" we know all about "two", because "two" is "one and one". We forget that we still have to make a study of "and". Secondary physics is the study of "and"—that is to say, of organisation.'

Just consider our own make-up. Each cell in our body consists of about eighty per cent water. (As H. G. Wells remarked, 'Even the Archbishop of Canterbury is eighty per cent water.') Besides the water each cell contains about 10^{10} (ten thousand million) macromolecules. Our brains alone contain 10^{10} cells; hence about 10^{20} macromolecules. Does anyone really believe that the physics of elementary particles, studied in isolation, explains and determines the continuing sense of identity, the continuing organisation of a complex animal or human brain and body? Yet this is the popular fallacy because the physics of most people is at least one hundred years out of date. You may not think this is a very important matter but here is a little story to emphasise it. Some time ago a friend of mine was having a conversation with a young man who hoped to marry his daughter. They had a long argument centring around this kind of problem, reductionism and so forth. He was getting more and more tired of this and he rather unfairly said, 'Oh, so you think of my daughter as a very large number of protons and electrons and macromolecules, etc., all organised by a series of complex electronic fluxes, do you?' And the young man said, 'Yes, I do.' And that ended the conversation for that evening; but he came back the next morning and said, 'I still think I was right in what I said last night but I must say it doesn't feel like it.' It's nice to know the two were married some two or three years ago and are living, as far as I know, very happily.

It seems that many people find this type of problem particularly acute in the light of statements, continually being made by so-called 'popularisers' of science, to the effect that the brain—and by implication, the mind—is nothing but a highly elaborate computer. It is the working assumption of neurophysiologists studying the brains of animals and men, that all conscious human activity and experience—choosing, seeing, believing, etc., has a correlate in corresponding neural activity. If all physical changes in the brain are determined by prior physical function, the future content of conscious experience would, in principle, be predictable from these factors. And so it might seem that our conviction of having free will might be an illusion.

But such a conclusion embodies a fallacy. It is the mechanism of thinking, not our experience of it, that may be explicable in the activity of the 10^{10} cells in our brains. The picture arrived at would, of necessity, leave out the internal knowledge that we each have as conscious beings. Not even a computer can contain within itself a complete and up-to-date representation of its current state. There is, in fact, no logical justification for dismissing the mental activities of our brains as mere 'by-products' of the operations of a stupendously complicated computer. We cannot, from the very nature of the case, explain away thereby our acquisition of knowledge of the external world nor our ability to make a personal choice. Whatever direction in which future advancement of knowledge concerning the action of the brain may go, it cannot have this consequence; for if it were true, none of our knowledge on any subject could be valid and so it could only be self-destructive.

To come to the effects of reductionist belief at the extreme end of the biological scale—on the mental health, indeed the sanity of modern man himself, Dr. Viktor Frankl, Professor of Psychiatry in the University of Vienna and widely known for his therapeutic work, finds that one of the major threats to health and sanity is what he calls the 'existential vacuum'; a world-wide phenomenon. More and more patients, in all parts of the world, crowd into the clinics and consulting rooms disrupted by a feeling of inner emptiness, a sense of total and absolute meaninglessness of their lives. And he believes that this is the direct outcome, the disastrous result, of the denial of value; of a widespread assumption that, since science in its technique is largely reductionist, reductionism is the only philosophy in which one can believe.

I recently heard one of the most distinguished theoretical chemists in this country, and indeed in the world, state that his own scientific drive is based upon two fundamental attitudes: 'a conviction of my own responsibility' and an 'awe at the beauty and harmony of nature'. It is these attitudes which have always been the mainspring of the scientific enterprise. But note that these are also very good reasons for being religious. And it has often been suggested, most notably I think by Whitehead in 1929, that science as we know it could not have arisen except against a background of centuries of Christian civilisation. For only a belief in the value of the natural order could have given the stimulus for the life-absorbing urge of the pioneer dedicated scientists to study the natural world against such overwhelming odds.

To turn again to reductionism: those reductionists who try to reduce life to physics usually try to reduce it to primitive physics—not to good physics. Good physics may turn out to be broad enough to contain life, to encompass life in its description, since good physics allows a vast field of possible descriptions; far more than any of us can at present envisage. There is no reason why living beings should be compared to primitive machines which don't make use of feedback. In others words, if we had a real understanding of the nature of physics today, or as it may become, there might be very little danger left in reductionism. And indeed if and when physics gets that far we may find that we have a unified science in which physics and biology are no longer separately distinguishable. As Whitehead said many years ago, biology is the study of the larger organisms and physics the study of the smaller ones. And that in a sense is true and I think Whitehead was envisaging—a possibility that would please me, naturally—that it is biology that will take over physics and not physics take over biology. But unfortunately the ordinary man's physics is still that of 100 or more years ago! Thus von Weiszaker says, 'the concept of the particle is itself just a description of a connection which exists between phenomena, and if I may jump from a very cautious and skilled language into strict metaphysical expression, I see no reason why what we call "matter" should not be in fact "spirit".' Thus physical theories and concepts portray not nature itself, but our knowledge of nature.

If reductionism were right in the sense that the mental, spiritual, artistic and ethical values which we experience really are in the electrons and other primary components of which the world is made—then all one can say is that they don't appear to be there. By the reductionist's view we are required to believe what we can in no way detect. By the moral and religious we are required to believe in a source of value added to, or injected into, the natural process as complexity develops, which we are totally unable to understand. Thus science properly understood really does withdraw its opposition to religion, in the sense defined just now, in that the essential basis of scientific activity involves a passionate belief in the value of striving towards a view of the universe as a single coherent whole.

Religious experience is similar in certain respects to that of science, as it is to that of art, in that it also develops through a systematic, reasoned structuring of those experiences through which we reach judgments and conclusions as to the value, worthwhileness and basic reality of certain aspects of our lives and thoughts; that is, the primacy of those question-begging entities we deal with under such terms as goodness, truth, beauty and love. Pure science cannot possibly enter into such antagonisms since it, itself, as I have tried to show, is engaged upon much the same quest. And indeed, religious people trying to find the good life and worthy objects of devotion are, or should be, trying out in faith their precepts and beliefs as guides and stays in the process of living; in much the same experimental way as scientists test hypotheses by experiment.

But of course science itself has a right and, indeed, a duty to comment and criticise where religious dogmas include beliefs about the physical world which appear incompatible with the accepted physical world-picture of the times. It is purely justifiable to point to the high improbability of such being true and to inquire whether such beliefs really are a necessarily integral part of the faith to which they belong.

Science is constantly exercising a refining and purifying role in this way, from which religion benefits beyond measure over the years, however unwelcome its comments may seem at the time. True religion has nothing to fear from science for man is, by his very nature, a philosophical, metaphysical and religious animal. As Dostoevsky says somewhere, 'Man needs the unfathomable and the infinite just as much as he needs the small planet which he inhabits.' Man's home is, in a very real sense, the whole universe and with nothing less can his understanding ultimately be content.

CHAPTER THIRTEEN

THE SPIRIT AND THE LAW

by the Right Honourable LORD DENNING,
Master of the Rolls

Your Vicar told me that the congregation consists of untheologically-minded students! Perhaps not quite the same as in the case of the bishop who went to the Temple Church where the lawyers congregate and the acoustics are not at all good. The verger said to the bishop, 'Pray, my lord, speak very clearly and distinctively because the agnostics here are terrible.'

If I were to choose a text this evening I would simply take St. Paul's words: 'The letter killeth but the spirit giveth life.' All through history you will see that the letter killeth. Do you remember the story of our Lord going through the cornfields and his disciples began to pluck the ears of corn on the Sabbath day and the Pharisees said to him, 'Why do your disciples do that which is not lawful on the Sabbath day?' And our Lord replied, 'The Sabbath was made for man and not man for the Sabbath.' All through those passages in the New Testament you will see the letter of the law being applied by the Jews: and each time our Lord replied, 'The spirit giveth life.' We see that conflict every day in our courts of law today. May I give you just one illustration? We had a case where a young doctor and his wife had just married and went to the South Seas. Before they went, each made his will. He said in his will, 'If I die first I leave all my property to you'; and she said, 'If I die first I leave all my property to you.' Each put in his or her will, 'If our deaths coincide, the property of each goes to his own relatives.' Those two went out in a little ship in the South Seas. After seven days nothing was heard of it. A little wreckage was found from which it could be seen the ship went down suddenly with all hands at once. No one could live for a second in those shark-ridden waters. Did their deaths 'coincide'? The majority of the court held they did not because there might be the fraction of a second between them. I say the *majority* of the court! When I was a judge at first instance sitting alone I could, and did, do justice. In a court of appeal of three, sometimes the chances of doing justice may be two to one against!

But you know this conflict between the letter and the spirit runs through our interpretation of the law. You will recall those words of Portia:

> *Tarry a little, there is one thing more—*
> *This bond doth not give thee one jot of blood,*
> *The words expressly are 'a pound of flesh':*
> *Take then thy bond, take thou thy pound of flesh,*
> *But if in the cutting it, thou dost shed*
> *One drop of Christian blood, thy lands and goods*
> *Are (by the laws of Venice) confiscate*
> *Unto the State of Venice.*

Portia invoked the letter in order to give life. Mr. Quintin Hogg, quite recently in the House of Commons, speaking on our court decisions about the gaming clubs (when the courts, some of them—not ours—had interpreted the gaming laws by the letter and so enabled these gaming clubs to flourish contrary to the intention of Parliament), said, 'For the lawyer the maxim must be the spirit killeth but the letter giveth life.' I would never subscribe to that view.

You heard in the lesson this evening the quotation from Romans, 'Love is the fulfilling of the law.' It was Archbishop William Temple who said this, 'Love in social life and in society finds its primary expression through justice.' This means in practice that each side should state its case as strongly as it can before the most impartial tribunal available with the determination to accept the award of a tribunal. At least that puts the two parties on a level and it is to that extent in accord with the command, 'Thou shalt love thy neighbour as thyself.' The judges consciously or subconsciously, when they properly develop our law, have applied our Christian precepts. Take the precept, 'Thou shalt love thy neighbour as thyself.' Listen to one of our great judges, over thirty years ago now, in a case—the lawyers here will know it—about a snail in a bottle of ginger beer. A man bought a bottle of ginger beer. He gave it to his wife. She drunk it and became ill. She brought an action against the manufacturer for negligence in allowing a snail to be in the bottle. On the previous law it seemed clear that the manufacturer was not liable. He had not made any contract with the wife. But Lord Atkin took the precept 'Thou shalt love thy neighbour as thyself' and said that in law it became, 'Thou shalt not injure thy neighbour.' To the lawyer's question, 'Who then is my neighbour?', the judge replied, 'Those persons whom I ought to have in mind when I am considering what may happen or the consequence of what I may do.'

In that case one of the greatest judges in our time formed legal principles on a Christian foundation. So also in regard to our great problem of race and colour. That problem came before the judges two hundred years ago in the days of slavery. A master brought a slave from Jamaica. In those days a slave was regarded as a chattel, like a piece of furniture. The slave wanted to stay in England. The master wanted to take him back to Jamaica. He held him in irons in a ship on the Thames. That slave brought before the judges the great writ of habeas corpus which protects the liberties of an individual against any unjust detention. Lord Mansfield, on that occasion, used these words, 'Every man who comes into England is entitled to the protection of the English law whatever oppression he may heretofore have suffered and whatever may be the colour of his skin. The air of England is too pure for any slave to breathe—let the black go free.' And he was set free. Only recently in Notting Hill some white youths of sixteen or seventeen years of age in a gang set upon any coloured man or boy they could find in the streets and were brought before Mr. Justice Salmon. In the ordinary way they would have been bound over and put on probation, or given six months. Mr. Justice Salmon sentenced them to five, six and seven years, and said, 'Everyone coming into this country is entitled to walk through our streets with his head erect and free from fear.' The law has proclaimed that there shall be no racial discrimination. It no doubt is right that we should have laws to prevent undue immigration. We have had cases recently in our court where youngsters coming from India or Pakistan have a right to come if they are the son of their fathers. But we have seen cases where some try all forms of deceit to get in. We must throughout the law keep the right spirit, 'Thou shalt love thy neighbour as thyself'; but, on the other hand, we must see that there are just laws so that our own community is protected.

Next is one of the problems of our time: the difference between sin and crime. Sin is that for which a man is accountable to God; crime is that for which he is accountable to the law and to society at large to be punished. That was brought home to me in a case in which I was concerned concerning suicide. What is suicide, or attempted suicide? Is it a sin or a crime? For centuries the law of England declared it was the most heinous crime of all—a man rushing into the presence of his Maker unasked. We had a case in which Major Rowlandson had insured his life for £80,000, and the policy was due to expire at three o'clock on a June afternoon. If he died before three o'clock he or his creditors would get £80,000; and if he died after three they would get nothing. At half past two in the afternoon he went to his solicitors in Chancery Lane and, after seeing them, at a quarter to three he left the office and called a taxi. He said to the taxi-driver, 'As you pass St. James's Palace clock look at the time and note it.' On his way to his flat in Albemarle Street the taxi-driver did so. He looked at the clock in St. James's Palace. It showed three minutes to three. As he went up St. James's Street he heard a shout. He stopped the taxi, got out, and there was Major Rowlandson dead—two minutes to three. Just in time, you may think. I appeared for the creditors and the executors of the dead man. I was led by Sir William Jowitt. We were faced with the proposition that 'suicide is a crime, a felony, and the most heinous crime of all'. No man could recover for a crime. To get over it we tried to say that he was of unsound mind, but the judge would not have it. He told the jury, 'Was not this the act of a gallant English gentleman killing himself for the sake of his creditors?' And so he was of sound mind. We took the case to the Court of Appeal. We took it to the House of Lords. I remember Sir William Jowitt left me to carry on at the end. He said, 'Cite to them Hamlet, you know, the grave-diggers, and so on.' So I did what I could, but it was of no avail. Suicide was the most heinous crime of all, and we lost. But now it is all altered by a statute a few years ago. Suicide is no longer a crime.

Attempted suicide is no longer a crime. It is a sin. I venture to think that in many of the problems in which we have to deal with today, whether it is homosexuality or abortion, or the taking of drugs, many of them are sins. Whether they should be ranked as crimes is a further step. They should be ranked as crimes only if they have their impact on society at large. But I would not carry the crime beyond that a man should only be guilty of a crime when he has a guilty mind —that is the Christian precept. You may have seen a case quite recently where a lady let out her house to tenants, and six months later there was found, in the rooms of one her tenants, cannabis and other drugs. Although she knew nothing of it, she was held guilty of managing a house in which people were in possession of drugs. The case is being much criticised. All I would say is that the Christian precept requires that a man should be guilty of a crime when he has a guilty mind. It is a wrong public policy which makes a person guilty of a crime when there is no guilty mind.

Then you may ask the question, 'What is justice?' That is a question many people far wiser than you or I have asked over the centuries. No one, as far as I know, has found a satisfactory answer. Plato asked it two thousand years ago, and could give no good answer. Justice is not a temporal thing. It is eternal. It is a thing of the spirit. The nearest approach to a definition that I can give is that justice is what the right-thinking members of the community believe to be fair. We all of us represent the right-thinking members of the community, trying as best we can to do what is fair. And in these days the judges have to try to do it, not only between man and man but between man and the State. Do you know that every judge in England on his appointment takes an oath and these are the words of it:

'I swear by Almighty God that I will do right to all manner of people after the laws and usages of this realm, without fear or favour, affection or ill-will.'

Take each phrase of it. 'I swear by Almighty God', hereby he affirms his belief in God, and hence in true religion. 'That I will do right', that I will do justice, not that I will do law. 'To all manner of people', rich or poor, capitalist or communist, Christian or pagan, black or white, to all manner of people will I do right. 'After the law and usages of this realm'; yes, it must be according to law. 'Without fear or favour, affection or ill-will', without fear of the powerful or favour of the wealthy; without affection for one side or ill-will towards another, I will do right.

It reminds us of the oath which the Queen herself takes at the Coronation. The Archbishop asks her, 'Will you to your power cause law and justice in mercy to be executed throughout your Dominions?' and the Queen answers, 'I will.' The judges are the delegates of the Queen for the purpose, to do law and justice in mercy. And how shall they be merciful unless they have something in them of that quality which, as Shakespeare says, 'droppeth like the gentle rain from heaven upon the place beneath'? Those precepts of the law fit in entirely with the precepts you find in the Bible. 'What doth the Lord require of thee' asked the prophet Micah, 'but to do justly, to love mercy and to walk humbly with thy God?' That is the spirit which should pervade all of us, the Spirit of God which reaches its highest and best when it tells us what is right and true and should be done. And we in the law should always try to bring into our work, all of us should try to bring into work, the spirit of understanding, the Christian precepts in which we have been brought up and which I hope we can carry on in this great country of ours.

AFRICA AND ENGLAND

CHAPTER FOURTEEN

ENGLAND: NAUGHT FOR YOUR DESIRE

by the Bishop of Stepney
(the Right Reverend TREVOR HUDDLESTON)

You understand that I have an assignment in speaking to you and that I was not the chooser of the subject that was given me. Nevertheless I am deeply thankful for the opportunity. Since I suppose—indeed I am pretty certain—that in these days G. K. Chesterton is a poet not much read, I must explain that the title of my address is taken from the same verse of his *Ballad of the White Horse*, as was the title of my earlier book:

> *I tell you naught for your comfort,*
> *Yea, naught for your desire,*
> *Save that the sky grows darker yet*
> *And the sea rises higher.*

Some thirteen years ago, just before I was recalled from South Africa after spending twelve and a half years there, I tried to record my own feelings and my own convictions about the meaning of life in that tortured country, and all I could say was that at least I wrote with some authority because of the length of time I had spent there; and in those days it was possible for someone with a white skin to move right in the heart of urban African society. And that is my only justification really for writing such a book. Since then, of course, very many books have been written about race and colour conflict both in South Africa and elsewhere and I am quite certain that if you were to read my book today you would feel that it was only too terribly familiar. But when I wrote it I was attempting to show that South Africa, by maintaining a policy of racial segregation—apartheid—was in fact making for future generations a crisis which could become a crisis on a world scale, and I was drawing upon a very local experience over a limited period of time to try to point to this crisis. And so I chose

the title that I did. 'I tell you naught for your comfort.'
Whether I was right or wrong, time alone will show. All I
can say is, that if I were to write that book again, although
I might alter quite a lot of the content of the actual historical
events which took place in my day, the only alteration I
could make in the substance of it would be to draw more
darkly the shadows. Tonight at the request of your Vicar I
am asked to speak to you about our own country and I've
chosen words from the same verse in Chesterton's poem but
I'm not attempting the same exercise. Obviously not, because
in fact whereas I was in South Africa for twelve and a half
years before writing a book about it, I've only been back in
this country for six months. The last eight years I have had
the privilege of working in a very poor area in a very poor
country—Tanzania. In fact it's only three months since I
began my new job as Bishop of Stepney in East London.
And therefore whatever else I speak from, I cannot claim to
speak from experience of this country and I want to make
that absolutely clear. And yet there are advantages as you
know, I think, in speaking when one's first impressions are
still sharp and defined, and so tonight I try to speak to you
about the state of this country as it makes its first impact
upon me after some twenty years on the continent of Africa;
first of all in a great environment, Johannesburg, and latterly
in a remote rural diocese whose people are all peasant
farmers and most of whom have no income or salary whatever, but live by what they can grow.

In attempting to do this I really do recognise the
dangers. In the first place I'm still terribly homesick for
Africa, for the place and for the people amongst whom I
have lived and worked. The only comparison I really can
make to my present condition is that of an amputation. One
has to learn to walk again. Looking back on the days when
one had two limbs makes one recognise how thrilling it was
to be able to move so swiftly. But walking or learning to
walk with an amputation is always a bore and sometimes a
great burden. So I speak to you recognising that I still really
have the better part of me in the land that I love most, and
that naturally will cast its light about what I say about this
country. So remember it. Certainly I do recognise, I hope,
the tremendous complexity of our society and the complexity
of its institutions and I hope I'm sufficiently aware of my

own limitations to know that I cannot speak with first-hand authority of the social order in which I now find myself. And again, as I think everybody recognises, it is a social order in revolution. I suppose that when the history of this particular generation comes to be written the note that will be struck most clearly will be that of the pace of social change in these last ten years, the fantastic pace and the continuing pace of social revolution all mixed up with scientific and technological revolution. And then lastly (and I hope I am being open with you), I do find the new job to which I have been called an utterly exhausting one; and when you are a little weary perhaps you see things with a slightly more jaundiced eye than if you are young and fresh, and I am only too well aware that I am neither. The limitations of middle age are now becoming only too apparent to me.

So having said all that, which is by way of a warning, I'd like to say just one or two things about the advantages of speaking to you about your own country at this moment. I do believe that having come from another continent, not just another country (and incidentally this is something which I think might well be remembered—the appalling condescension of people who talk of Africa as if it were a country and not a continent of countries), that having come from another continent to this one I think there is an advantage in the very fact of contrast. Contrast does give clearer vision than familiarity. One isn't yet, I hope, submerged by established attitudes or by the establishment itself, and further as a Christian—and even bishops can sometimes claim that name —I am confronted with issues, with problems and opportunities alike, which in fact didn't even exist before I went to Masasi, but which now have to be recognised and used. I went before the Vatican Council and before the great ecumenical movement had so to speak broken upon the Western Church. I have come back into an open Church, though, alas, a very strongly established part of it; and I've come back to a society in which secularism or if you prefer it secularisation is the supreme quality of life.

> *I tell you naught for your comfort,*
> *Yea, naught for your desire,*
> *Save that the sky grows darker yet*
> *And the sea rises higher.*

The sky and the sea—those are the two symbols that I want to speak about tonight; and I suppose that since John Robinson's *Honest to God* it's a bit dangerous to use imagery at all. One is almost certain to be accused of talking about God 'out there' or 'out here' or 'out somewhere'. But I'm going to risk this, because my assignment is a complicated one as well as being a very direct challenge; England today as seen by a Christian returning. Please don't imagine that I think that my personal views are significant, but I do think that national self-awareness is supremely important and sometimes an individual's views may have the effect of bringing to a point of awareness the submerged thoughts and feelings of many millions: and so I take 'the sky' to symbolise everything that is present in our national life that dims our vision. 'The sky grows darker yet.' And I take 'the sea' to symbolise all that is present in our national life that threatens to overwhelm man as man.

When I was young I remember being moved, perhaps even thrilled at that time, by a poem which was on everybody's lips just after the First World War. As I read it now, and its words have often come singing through my veins, I think how totally impossible it would be for our generation —meaning yours and mine together—to write such words of England today.

And think, this heart, all evil shed away,
A pulse in the eternal mind, no less
Gives somewhere back the thoughts by England given;
Her sights and sounds; dreams happy as her day;
And laughter learnt of friends; and gentleness,
In hearts at peace, under an English heaven.

The key has changed. 'The sky grows darker yet.' The first thing that strikes anybody like myself coming back from Africa today is not concerned so much with light as with noise; the actual noise of life in our society. It may be said that I am exaggerating because I live on Commercial Road in Stepney, which I believe is the busiest road in England. And therefore not unnaturally I am aware of the fact that for twenty-four hours out of twenty-four, articulated lorries, fire engines, ambulances and a perpetual rout of traffic is passing up and down below my window. But it isn't really that noise that worries me, it's the noise of words and words and words. It's the effect of living perpetually with a flood of information pouring over us from radio and television and the press so that it is almost physically impossible to stand back and hear what is being said, still less to stand back and understand it.

> *What is this life, if full of care*
> *We have no time to stand and stare?*

It isn't the standing and the staring which is important; it is the opportunity for stillness. Where do we find this opportunity in England today? I'm certain that the effect of this noise, in whichever sense you take it, upon human freedom and human dignity is shown in the superficiality of judgment and the shallowness of the kind of wisdom that we are receiving. This must be disastrous for man as man; and for those who believe in God, there is a deeper disaster. 'Be still and know that I am God.' If we lose the capacity for stillness (and I believe we are rapidly losing it), then we are in very great peril of losing the meaning of our existence as the children of God.

And connected with noise, after the pace of life in Africa I find there is a fantastic obsession with speed and movement for its own sake. Again perhaps I am jaundiced because I have to drive myself through the City of London countless times during every week. But a whole society in such rapid movement and constant flux, what really is it all about? What are we saving time for? What does it really mean, this lust to overtake at every possible opportunity? Does it mean that we are passionately desirous of arriving at our work? I am bound to say that the state of industrial relations in this country doesn't reflect that attitude. Does it mean that we are really urgently in need of leisure and therefore are escaping from work? The fact that we spend £2,000 million a year on gambling does suggest that our leisure isn't very profitable either. Or does it mean that we are caring to get home to our families? Well, the Provost of one of your own colleges said quite recently, 'Far from being the basis of a good society the family with its narrow privacy and tawdry secrets is the source of all our discontent.' So I can't think it's that either. Nevertheless this fact of pace, of movement, of totally undirected speed seems to me to be very, very alarming, and certainly contrary to an awareness of divine realities. 'Come ye apart and rest awhile, for there are many coming and going.'

We have the Lord's authority for thinking that such rest is necessary. But most of all, to one coming back from Africa, there is a deep and bitter sense of the loss of community. Harvey Cox in *The Secular City* quotes another American writer, Jane Jacobs, as saying this:

> 'Nobody can keep open house in a great city. Nobody wants to ... Cities are full of people with whom, from your viewpoint or mine or any other individual's, a certain degree of contact is useful or enjoyable; but you do not want them in your hair. And they do not want you in their's either.'

On which Cox comments:

> 'Theologians would do well to appreciate this characteristically urban "togetherness" ... and to see in its impersonal, even anonymous inter-relatedness an authentic form of *corporate human existence* in the urban epoch.'

What connection is there between 'a certain degree of contact' and the reality of community of the common life? The fragmentation of families because of housing shortages and housing development; the desperate isolation and loneliness of the old, because they are no longer able to be accommodated with their children and grandchildren in the new tower blocks or the new towns of our country; the equal isolation and frustration of the very young; because there is nowhere to play and no group to play with: I suppose you can describe all this as 'corporate human existence'. But God help us if it is supposed to be a desirable pattern of corporate human life! Someone like myself is familiar with the basic structure of African society—the extended family, and all that that means in terms of caring, so that, for instance, in the part of Africa I have just come from, an orphanage would be a total impossibility because there are no children who do not belong. An old people's home would be a total impossibility because of course the aged 'belong' and are the most honoured members of the family. Cox's analysis of our society which seems to be accepted whole-heartedly by modern theologians is to someone like me depressingly bleak and his commendation of it is, I believe, totally misguided. But the facts are inescapable. We are creating for ourselves in this land, in fact we have already created, a social order of almost unbearable loneliness. And 'it is not good for man to be alone'.

'The sea rises higher.' It would, of course, be possible to expand on all the themes I have mentioned, and many more. But I want to turn from sky to sea; from the things which obscure our vision to the things which threaten to overwhelm us as human beings in society. And, again, the choice is wide. No doubt my choice is conditioned by my own circumstances, but in any case the symbol of sky and the symbol of sea meet together on a horizon.

To one returning from one of the newly independent countries of Africa, as I have said, a very poor country, yet engaged, out of its own poverty, in tremendous development and nation-building projects, it is the introspectiveness of English society and of English political and economic attitudes whch hit one hardest between the eyes.

The great cry goes up for more 'participation in demo-cratic processes'. The protests and the sit-ins and the demon-strations are the outward expression of this. And yet, to the outsider (and I still put myself in this category, perhaps because I do not want to be inside?) there appears to be a positive obsession in our country today with the idea of self-interest; and this at every level of national life. The standard of living—that blessed phrase—is used to cover every possible form of greed and selfishness. The standard of living must be raised every year, every month, every week, every day—why? Because the luxury we already have is not enough. It is to me totally impossible to say of the wel-fare state that at this moment of contrasting standards in the world in which we live we are a country still in need of higher standards of living. Yet because we do say this, the test of government is the balance of payments situation. Social goals like health, education, penal reform, housing, everything must be abandoned or subordinated to this national lust after superfluous comfort. International policies; aid to under-developed countries; war or peace in Vietnam,

Nigeria, the Middle East; all these things are subject more to Treasury control than to any idea of national morality.

It is possible (and indeed it happens all the time), in such a mood to defend all policies and none on the ground of political pragmatism and even to be believed, so that on the one hand, negotiations can take place and agreement can be contemplated with an illegal white minority government in Rhodesia, and on the other, aid can be withdrawn from a desperately poor country like Tanzania. Why? Because of a disagreement over the pensions of former English colonial administrators. The list of such double talk and double dealing can be lengthened almost indefinitely and stretches back far beyond the term of office of the present government. The root cause of all such attitudes and policies is, I believe, a sickness of the soul of our country. It is not just that, as Dean Acheson told us in a moment of truth, we have lost an Empire and not discovered a role. It is that we are so busy with our own selfish concerns that we can't be bothered to look for a role or to seek to fulfil it.

Because the Christian Church is set firmly in the midst of this situation—and must be so, because its Lord 'emptied himself and became of no reputation' and washed men's dirty feet—it is inescapably the task of the Church both to prophesy and to heal. In the whole field of race relations, for example, both at the international level and within our own country we as Christians have an unparalleled opportunity for moral choice and the proclamation of moral obligations. I want to quote you two sentences from a recent book by an American Negro leader of the Black Panther Movement because I believe they are extremely important for us to hear:

'The rebellion of the oppressed peoples of the world, along with the Negro revolution in America, has opened a way to a new evaluation of history, a re-examination of the role played by the white race since the beginning of European expansion. The positive achievements are also there in the record, and future generations will applaud them. But there can be no applause now, not while the master still holds the whip in his hand.'

(Eldridge Cleaver, *Soul on Ice*.)

Here is a moral issue of absolute and perhaps final significance for humanity. 'A division on race or colour lines is inescapably more dangerous than one on ideological lines.' The possibility of race war is a more immediate possibility. Now it can be said—and said with truth—that the Church has spoken unequivocally more often than not on this issue in recent years. Racism has been condemned by the Pope, the World Council of Churches and by the Lambeth Fathers and by individual Christian leaders and Church Councils over and over again. Both in the United States and South Africa bishops, clergy and laity have borne a brave personal witness, often involving deportation or imprisonment. Indeed it is significant surely that the fight against racism has, in the person of Martin Luther King, provided the Church of our day with its own particular martyr. 'Deep down in our non-violent creed,' he once said, 'is the conviction that there are some things so dear, some things so precious, some things so eternally true that they are worth dying for'—and he died! There is every indication in our country that, very soon on this issue of race, Christians will have to stand up and be counted. Do let us remember that at that moment the divisiveness of Christ's sword will be much more apparent than the comfort of Christ's peace.

And yet, when all is said and done, the main task of the Church is to be the Church. What does this mean? This for Christians is the question of the moment. The Church—what is it? An institution, strongly built, as complex as any other institution in the world? A vehicle for evangelism by word, by print, by television and every channel open to us? A refuge for all the drop-outs, the meths drinkers and the lonely? I suppose it is all of these. But, fundamentally, the definition of the Church of GOD is a simple thing; so simple that we, with our highly sophisticated technologically inspired, scientifically moulded view of life can today hardly see or believe it.

'None of them said that anything was his own. They had all things common.' What was it, really, which drew men to the Lord in the dawn days of the Christian Church? When the paganisms, the secularisms and the false gods pressed in upon them with unimaginable force; when the Church itself was just scattered groups of simple men and women, many of them slaves—the dung of the earth—what was it?

How could they compel men to this allegiance? Was it their oratory? Did they walk secretly the corridors of power? Had they some some esoteric mysteries to communicate to that world of alienated humanity? It was none of these things. 'They had all things common.' It was the existence of a community, of a worshipping, believing, steadfast community which compelled men to believe and to move out of their twilight into glory. Did I say 'A community'? If I did I am wrong! The Church is The Community for man, or it is nothing. The Church is the reflection in time of the mystery of Godhead itself, of a love which can only find expression in mutuality, in the common life. So I understand it.

The modern world, and our country within it, is desperately seeking new forms, new patterns of life that will give meaning to its structures and institutions. It ought to find these things supremely—perhaps only—in one place: in GOD'S community, the One Holy Catholic and Apostolic Church, the Church which is the common people of GOD but which is also the vehicle of hope in a disturbed and revolutionary period of time; the vehicle of hope. However great a revolution we are experiencing in the secular world the Church itself is fundamentally and essentially a revolutionary community. It is a community which turns the world upside down, because it asserts the supreme value of the individual person to consist first of all in a recognition of the fact that he is God's creature and secondly in the recognition of the fact that he cannot fulfil himself as a person outside the common life.

What a challenge! What an opportunity! Certainly there is nothing to be depressed or gloomy about in being a Christian today.

> I tell you naught for your comfort,
> Yea, naught for your desire,
> Save that the sky grows darker yet
> And the sea rises higher.
> Night shall be thrice night over you,
> And heaven an iron cope.
> Do you have joy without a cause,
> Yea, faith without a hope?

CHAPTER FIFTEEN

AFRICA: DAMN YOUR CHARITY

by the Reverend STANLEY BOOTH-CLIBBORN,
formerly of the Lincoln City Centre Team Ministry,
now Vicar of Great St. Mary's

This century has been called by a good many names; the
age of the bomb, the age of the refugee, and others. I would
like to suggest another title: 'the age of the march'. In
recent years, our newspapers have been filled with stories
about marches protesting about this, that and the other social
evil. Such marches have often produced effective slogans,
paraded on banners through the streets of our cities. Slogans
on banners can of course be dangerous. In Uganda in the
years before independence, the magnificent slogan 'WE ARE
FED UP WITH THE BRITISH GOVERNMENT' was carried by the
marchers on two banners side by side. This was all right
until the banner bearers were separated, and one lot continued to hold high the slogan 'UP WITH THE BRITISH
GOVERNMENT' to their considerable discomfiture!

There is one kind of march we haven't seen for at least a
generation. We hope we never see it again in this country.
But it isn't all that many years ago that long lines of ragged
men, with pinched faces and crumbling shoes, set off on the
long journey to London to confront those in the seats of
power with the plight of the unemployed.

History tells us that on the way they were helped by well-
meaning people with hot soup and bread. Clothes and other
necessities were sent to their families. But such well-meaning
people must have been puzzled, even hurt, by one slogan
on their banners, a slogan which has rung through history.
'DAMN YOUR CHARITY—WE WANT JUSTICE.'

Things have changed in Britain. I believe that a major
factor in this change has been that this slogan, and all the
wealth of meaning behind it, has been generally accepted as
a social philosophy in our land. It is now accepted that it is
the right of wage-earners to a job and a decent wage—that

people should not be expected to live on bits of charity doled out from the tables of the rich. Although people are critical of the small minority who abuse the Welfare State, the philosophy behind this provision is accepted by those in all political parties. Don't for one moment suppose that I am saying that no one in Britain lives in poverty. This would make nonsense of all the work of bodies such as Shelter in holding before our eyes the four million people who live in sub-standard houses, or the Child Poverty Action Group in alerting us to the needs of large families in twilight areas. Yesterday in Lincoln we had a consultation on this whole question in which, among other speakers, Tony Lynes of the Child Poverty Action Group, brought to our attention yet again the miserable conditions in which some seven million of our fellow-countrymen live.

But let's face it, Western Europe is as much an island of affluence in the middle of a hungry world, as were the wealthy suburban areas through which the unemployed passed in the hungry 1930s on their way to the seats of power. What has happened in our affluent society is that poverty has ceased to affect the majority of people. If you accept Mr. Lynes's definition of those 'who do not have the necessary minimum level of resources to participate fully in the life of society', then this now applies to the minority. But it is all the more difficult to solve, especially as they are concentrated in the very worst housing areas.

Poverty is a relative concept. It depends on the society in which you live. And it is a shame to us that we have such conditions in the midst of plenty. But a poor person in Britain is wealthy when compared with the way of life—if it can be called that—of many in Asia and Africa.

I would like to suggest to you that this slogan 'Damn your charity—we want justice' is now coming as an even louder cry from the developing nations of Asia and Africa. As my own experience of eleven years in East Africa has perhaps given me a foot in both worlds, let me speak principally of that vast continent. Africa is crying out—'Damn your charity —we want justice'!

This cry is finding an echo in the hearts and minds of some people in Britain. It is encouraging to find on coming back that people are prepared to raise considerable sums for such bodies as Oxfam and Christian Aid for development in Asia and Africa. It is still more encouraging to find all over the country, little groups springing up who see that the problem cuts a great deal deeper than the comparatively small amounts which we contribute whether in private or government aid. It cuts deep into the field of politics and the terms of trade. But not many people see it this way. One noted popular political philosopher of recent times has summed up the view of many in this way:

> Wot I say is we British 'ave given all the best bits away—the places on the map what was coloured red. The best bits, I mean. There's all them wogs sitting out there in the sun, and there's us over 'ere in the *** rain and fog and snow, catching colds and bronchitis. If anyone needs medical aid, it's us and not them Africans and Vietnams. Bronchitis is a bigger killer than bombs, too. Yer get all these flag sellers tramping round the streets wiv all their good causes. But you don't see anybody marchin' wiv Ban the Bronch signs to help us ...

I wouldn't like to be the Christian Aid or Oxfam collector to call on Alf Garnett!

Is Alf exceptional? I'm afraid not. Public opinion polls have shown clearly that in times of economic stress, the first thing most people would like to cut is overseas aid, even though this runs at the pathetically low figure of just over one per cent of our national income. And as for giving, including private investment, to Oxfam, Christian Aid, etc., at the last count this totalled about 3s. 4d. per head a year compared with about £24 spent on tobacco alone. Surely we in this country are a long way from taking seriously the problems of developing countries! The late John F. Kennedy's words have a hollow sound:

> Never before has man had such a capacity to control his own environment, to end thirst and hunger, to conquer poverty and disease, to banish illiteracy and massive human misery. We have the power to make this the best generation of mankind or to make it the last.

We don't look at Africa in the spirit of those challenging words. We tend to think of this vast continent as a land of mud huts and misery—the kind of misery you can do nothing about. In fact it is a continent on the march. But the marchers need the help of those who believe in justice and not charity. Moreover, there is a close parallel between the conditions in Britain many years ago and our world today. As a recent U.N. report put it:

> The Victorian Society bore a family resemblance to our deeply divided modern world economy. The gap was growing more and more absolute between the income and comforts of the rising industrial and financial groups and the blank misery of the labouring classes. Moreover a certain hopelessness hung over efforts to improve conditions.

All this has changed dramatically in Britain today. I believe that the Christian faith has had a great deal to do with the change. We are not prepared to tolerate these inequalities in our own society because of our view of man largely, though of course not entirely, fostered by the Christian faith. Other factors have contributed to the diminution of poverty such as our increasing tempo of technological change. But our view of man has been dominant. What is now needed is to see this on a world scale.

After one leave in Britain, my wife and I had returned and we were moving up the long 300-mile road through the bush country from Mombasa to Nairobi. We stopped the car miles from anywhere to settle the children for the night and far down the road came a distant figure on a bicycle. We could hear singing. As he drew nearer, we could see that he was an African dressed in ragged shorts and shirt, and he turned off down a track into the bush, but not before we heard the song coming clearly across the evening air. If we had been expecting some attractive Taita folk tune, we were disappointed. The words were: 'We're all going on a summer holiday.' He was living in the transistor age, and this was then top of the pops! The world is one as never before. The Christian churches have a great part to play in making people conscious of this fact, for it is implicit in the thought of the Bible. The great Jesuit theologian and scientist Teilhard de Chardin has spoken to our generation most movingly on this theme:

> In the course of a few generations, all sorts of economic

and cultural links have been forged around us and they are multiplying in geometric progression ... Nowadays over and above the bread which to simple Neolithic man symbolised food, each man demands his daily ration of iron, copper and cotton, of electricity, oil and radium, of discoveries, of the cinema and of international news. It is no longer a simple field however big, but the whole earth which is required to nourish each one of us ... Is this not like some great body which is being born ... ?

Teilhard goes on to speak of *love* as alone 'capable of uniting living beings in such a way as to complete and fulfil them, for it alone takes them and joins them by what is deepest in themselves.'

Love and justice march together as the teachings of Jesus so abundantly show. You cannot have one without the other. It is no good talking sentimentally about love towards the new and hungry nations of the earth unless we are prepared to recognise the *justice* of their demands. This is an uncomfortable process. But it is there in the Christian faith. It means the effort to understand, even when as a nation someone kicks us in the teeth. Of course it is unpleasant to be called 'a humbled toothless bulldog'. Of course it would be nice if people were grateful for all the money and help we sent to them. But men who want justice are not particularly grateful and this is a fact of experience.

This is a plea for understanding the new nations of Africa and for the kind of action from our side which can help in meeting their needs. The emergence of so many new nations in half a generation is perhaps the most dramatic revolution in world history. When I think of the colour of the map of the continent when I arrived in Nairobi compared with the situation when I left last year, it staggers the imagination. For young Africa, this is an exciting time full of possibilities. As we know, others in the continent have naturally had some fears and reservations, 'Why do you Europeans always talk as though the world is coming to an end?' said one African student during a meeting. 'For us, it is only just beginning.'

Please don't think that I am claiming that the actions of these new governments are beyond reproach. Christian leaders now find themselves in the position of criticising new governments composed of indigenous Africans in the same way that they opposed the actions of colonial or white supremacist regimes in the past. Bishop Trevor Huddleston once protested publicly against preventive detention in Tanzania and pointed out that human rights were the same in Tanzania as in South Africa where he had made himself unpopular on the same grounds. But such actions need understanding, as the leaders of the new nations struggle with the giant enemies of poverty, ignorance and disease.

As to action, there is still a vital need for the kind of help which goes through bodies such as Christian Aid and Oxfam. But the deeper question is related to the justice of the terms of trade in a world of such gross inequalities. Perhaps to some of you here, the call to action may well include consideration of the possibility that you might go to Africa. These new nations, much as they may resent the fact, are still overwhelmingly dependent on the skills of expatriates, especially in medicine and education.

Why should we listen to this cry for justice? After all, charity, in the sense in which we now use the word, is given when we feel like it. The demand for justice is inescapable once we accept it. I discussed this with a group of grammar school boys recently and asked them why we should help. After a long pause, one boy said, 'I suppose it's because we're all human, really.' That seems to me to be as good an answer as any. But some of us might wish to go further and to give the kind of depth to the answer which only faith can give. It is because 'God has made of one blood all nations to dwell on the earth'. It is because Christ has taught us to care.

CHAPTER SIXTEEN

PRISONERS OF HOPE

by the Reverend COLIN MORRIS,
Minister of Wesley's Chapel,
formerly Special Adviser to President Kaunda

'To your stronghold, you prisoners of hope.'
Zechariah 9:12

I was sitting in Lusaka International Airport the other day reflecting somewhat gloomily about the present state of Africa—undeclared war in Arab Africa, post-war wound-licking in Nigeria, civil and religious strife in Chad and the Sudan, and now an iron shutter crashing down in Rhodesia to cut off White Africa from the rest of the continent. Things looked so unpromising; yet at that moment there came unbidden into my mind this phrase from Zechariah—Prisoners of Hope. So my text for this sermon chose itself.

There can now be little doubt that the confrontation between black and white Africa has assumed the character of a Greek tragedy in which resolution only emerges from the far side of cataclysm. And in this tragedy, the main protagonists seem so committed to acting out a ritual destiny that it would not be inappropriate to call them 'prisoners'.

The white minority governments of Southern Africa and their supporters are prisoners of despair but not of pessimism. There is a buoyancy, a cocksureness in their ability to buck history that is quite breathtaking. All the same, they *are* prisoners of despair ...

When you are compelled to weave barbed wire around yourself as a protection against your fellow-citizens, your security is a form of imprisonment—you can only shut others out at the price of shutting yourself in ...

When you are committed to a doctrine of history so cock-eyed that in comparison *Alice in Wonderland* reads as sombrely as Bradshaw's *Railway Guide* ...

When highly intelligent people running a technologically

advanced society, the moment they lift their noses out of
their slide-rules, revert to a philosophy of life which resounds
to the rattle of ox-wagon wheels and the roar of Zulu hordes
—a philosophy shored up by phoney anthropology, men-
dacious statistics and a crude mysticism of blood—to believe
that lot, you have to do such violence to your intellect and
integrity that despair seems too mild a word ...

When you have such a chronic distrust of your fellow-
citizens of a different colour that you dare not place yourself
at their mercy; when you have so little confidence in the
justice of your past dealings with them that you live in
terror that one day you may be on the receiving end of the
treatment you have handed out to them for centuries—then
you are prisoners of despair.

When you dare not dance to the brave music being made
in other parts of Africa (and in spite of Nigeria, there *is*
brave, brave music being made in Africa); when you cannot
give due credit to the tremendous achievements of the new
nations of Africa but must exult in their set-backs, jeer at
their triumphs and rejoice in their agonies or else give the
lie to the philosophy of black depravity upon which you
have staked your existence—then brave, buoyant and tough
as you may be, you are trapped in a prison of despair.

In the drama of Southern Africa, the prisoners of optimism
are represented by the British government and her Western
allies. The convolutions of recent British policy towards
Africa are so opaque to the light of reason that the ordinary
man must conclude they are motivated by a dark machiavel-
lian subtlety which masquerades with brilliant success as
plain stupidity.

In particular, in its handling of the U.D.I. crisis, the
British government has fallen victim to what might be called
the Houdini Syndrome; you know—'Tie us in a thousand
chains and throw us over the Niagara Falls and in a trice
we shall be free!'—inviting mounting complications in order
to demonstrate virtuosity in overcoming them. Optimism,
pathetic optimism! 'There'll be no U.D.I.' 'All right, there
has been U.D.I. but it will all be over in a fortnight.' 'Well,
all right, they've survived the first year but our sanctions will
get them down sooner or later.' And so every creak in Salisbury is heralded in Whitehall as the first stone in a land-
slide which will sweep away the Smith regime.

The optimism of our government is compounded of unconscionable pride and utter unrealism. Their lack of understanding of white settler psychology is limitless. Did they seriously believe that the Smith Government would accept the *Tiger* and *Fearless* proposals and obligingly commit political suicide? Would the Labour government agree to constituency boundary changes which must produce a Tory majority till the end of time? Yet they expect Mr. Smith to implement a constitution whose ultimate result must be to rob him and his supporters of political power for ever and are hurt and disappointed when he refuses! Optimism! Pathetic optimism!

These prisoners of optimism are hard-headed realists about their own political prospects but expect others to be hopeless idealists about theirs. And in the same category I suppose we must count groups like the M.C.C. who think that the South African government arranges its affairs according to the laws of cricket, and that if you give the Springboks a rattling good time at Lords they will dash off back to Pretoria advocating a change to the good old British way of life—forgetting that South Africans turned their backs on the good old British way of life sixty years ago so that they would never have to rub shoulders with their coloured brethren in cricket pavilions.

Indeed, in the present state of race relations in Britain, there is grave danger that the Springboks might take back with them quite the wrong message, and having observed the sorry spectacle of Kenyan Asians waving British passports as they are propelled like yo-yos back and forth through the upper air might conclude that there's something to be said after all for honest-to-God apartheid.

The reason why both prisoners of despair and of optimism cannot make an adequate response to the situation in Southern Africa is that they ignore two theological dimensions of all political problems.

1. The radical nature of sin

When I left theological college I did not set much store by all this Christian talk about sin, but after fifteen years of involvement in African politics I am convinced that sin is a reality we ignore at our peril. Nations, racial groups and political parties do not repent by a simple rational process of analysing their past errors. There is a deep and all-pervasive corruption of the will at work within the body politic; and the prisoners of optimism in particular compound the old Marxist error of assuming that history itself is redemptive and that if it goes off course it is self-correcting on the basis of some moral or political or economic gyroscope built into it. They ignore the warning of our Lord in the parable of the wheat and the tares that history is morally ambiguous—every extension of good becoming the springboard for new possibilities of evil.

2. The grace of God

There is in operation in the political field a creative factor which does not spring naturally out of man's make-up or from his economic arrangements and political programmes—a factor that I can only describe as the operation of the grace of God. It unsnarls log-jams, spans unbridgeable gulfs, and resolves apparent deadlocks. I have seen this happen too often in concrete political situations ever to believe that talk about the grace of God is pious cant. It operates through men of affairs who make surprising renunciations and unpredictable sacrifices; who have unaccountable changes of mind and of heart and as a consequence the stalemate of eyeball to eyeball diplomacy is broken and mankind gets on the move again.

Prisoners of hope, who are the third group of protagonists in the Southern African drama, take due account of both these theological dimensions, though they may not dress them up in such fancy terminology. By so doing, they are preserved from the fundamental heresy of liberal politics—which is the belief that any international problem is soluble at a given point in time provided we put more elbow grease, more dedication and more ingenuity into its resolution. In fact, there are certain international problems which at any moment in history are strictly insoluble. I believe the problem of achieving justice for all the peoples of Southern Africa is, at the present time, totally intractable, and, paradoxically, the possibility of hope depends upon coming to terms with this hard fact.

The prisoner of hope can live with an intractable problem without lying down under it and cursing a capricious fate that it is beyond his present capacity to resolve. He knows that there are certain times which are the days of small things, just as there are others which are days of grand strategies. And in the day of small things, it is often by very tiny hinges that great weights are moved.

Africa is rich in prisoners of hope because she has often had to live in the day of small things through lack of technical resources and scientific sophistication, because of the dead weight upon her of superior alien cultures. Yet she has also seen mountains moved, deserts blossom and has lived out the miracles of nationhood and human survival against all odds. So there is no doubt that Africa will evolve a strategy of hope for dealing with this intractable problem at the southern tip of the Continent, and those who wish to identify themselves with her struggle would do well to share it.

Let me briefly sketch out three of the possible dimensions of such a strategy of hope.

1. *The ability to live in the present as though the future were already here.*

In Christian theology hope is always linked with the *parousia* and the scholars tell me that *parousia* means both what is present and what is coming. Now there is in African experience and thought-forms a sort of profane or secular or at least overtly non-Christian manifestation of *parousia*. For example, those of you who have tried to learn a Bantu language will know that present and future tenses are often hopelessly jumbled up. This has carried over into African politics. The peoples of Africa have a capacity for living in the present as though the future were already here which we in the West have lost, I think, because materialism supplies us with a bewildering variety of artefacts which provide a kind of barrier against the future—the material ballast that prevents us from packing our bags and getting on the move. If in a rich world, however, your only wealth is hope, it is amazing the ease with which you can smash through the metaphysical barrier between present and future.

Let me give you three illustrations of this.

At this moment in Mozambique there are large tracts of this Portuguese territory controlled by the Africa freedom movement—Frelemo. Inside an area honeycombed by Portuguese troops they have set up their own administration, organised schools and hospitals, and even their own police force. Frelemo's hold upon the area is fragile and should they be caught the price they will pay is a grievous one. But they steadfastly refuse to live in a depressing present and insist upon moulding their life in conformity with the future.

There are whites in Southern Africa who at great personal cost show a majestic contempt for apartheid. They will have nothing to do with the pass laws or the Group Areas Act; they are determined not to be cut off from their coloured brethren. They are living out the future in the midst of a cruel present and are paying sorely for the privilege.

In 1960, a great man—Kenneth David Kaunda—now President of the Republic of Zambia, then a nationalist leader on the run, sat in my house and sketched on a piece of paper a structure of government for a non-existent state to be called Zambia. He also put marks on a map where schools and hospitals were to be built. At this time, the peoples of Zambia were trapped in the Federation of Rhodesia and Nyasaland which seemed invincible in its power to hold up their constitutional advance. Those of us who sympathised with President Kaunda were beside ourselves with frustration: he, on the other hand, sat quietly administering on paper a non-existent state. Cynics might have sneered that he was like a child playing with soldiers, but when I drive now through Zambia and pass those very schools which were once pencil marks on a map I realise the extent to which the African people have been preserved from this corrosive pessimism which makes Westerners scale down their visions to the point of what is practically possible at a given moment.

All over Africa prisoners of hope are living out the future in the midst of an unpromising present, some of them at great cost. But they will change the texture of history.

2. *A willingness to operate the small hinges by which great weights move.*

Every night Rhodesian Africans slip back into their own country and engage Rhodesian forces in unequal combat. Their armament is derisory, their numbers are pathetic, their losses are terrifying. But they have made a decision which we liberals in the West, sympathetic to their plight, baulk at. They have seen that there are certain situations where the only hinge that moves great weights is force. And in so far as Christians wish to identify themselves with freedom struggles in Africa, Asia and Latin America, this is one nettle they will have to grasp. It may be a sad thing, but in the 20th century violence is one of the most important mechanisms of social and political change—a strictly temporary but sometimes effective solution to the problem of justice. Violence, to put it in Dantean terms, may well not establish a paradise but it can destroy an inferno.

This is not a palatable subject for Christians and it is understandable why we do not wish to give house-room to the possibility that it might be right to make, under certain conditions, a positive affirmation of the value of violence. Without doubt this is a theological issue in comparison with which every other theological issue of our day pales into insignificance. The only sizeable group of Christians at the present time who have evolved a theology of violence are pacifists. I admit the validity of their vocation and admire their witness to an ideal law of the Kingdom, but I do not believe that they articulate the only Christian position on this issue. Christian non-pacifists have, on the whole, avoided articulating their position, overcome by distaste at what they may be required to do to their fellow-men. This is understandable; but it will not do.

There is urgent need for a resumption of the dialogue between Christian pacifists and non-pacifists in the light of two realities of our day—nuclear weapons and revolution as an instrument of justice—which have rendered the old arguments and counter arguments irrelevant. In particular, those Christians who believe that the use of force can be squared with the Gospel, have an obligation to formulate a theology of violence which will lay down the conditions under which its use is permissible.

Because force is sometimes the only hinge about which great weights can be moved we have got to bring the issue out into the open. We are entitled to say that we will have none of it or that under certain conditions its use is justified, but we are not entitled to adopt a position of soggy neutrality and pretend that the widespread ferment of our day is not happening. If non-pacifists have an obligation to explore in detail the conditions in which the use of force is permissible, pacifists have also the duty of taking a long,

hard look at oppressive regimes such as those of Southern
Africa and offer a viable political strategy for achieving justice without the use of violence.

3.   *The necessity for bringing to bear the moral pressure
     of the whole of mankind upon any one part of it.*

When we have finished bemoaning the grip of tribalism
upon Africa and of pointing up the lessons of the tragedies
of the Congo and Nigeria, it is still true that the spirit of
internationalism has taken a greater hold in Africa in two
decades than in three hundred years of European history.
When the seventh wealthiest country in Africa is prepared
to enter into economic union with a number of poorer states
knowing that she will end up paying most of the bills while
they get most of the benefits, talk of African internationalism
is not just pious idealism.

In a number of ways, my stay in Africa has made it impossible for me to think in terms of any allegiance less embracing than all mankind. I can see no virtue in blind patriotism
and no realism in ecclesiastical affiliations. I have come to
believe that anything, however worth while it may seem in
itself, which cuts me off from my fellow-human beings, is
evil. And this is not a vague, visionary sentiment. We are
living in a time when prisoners of hope in every nation under
the sun have become conscious of a common history and
common experience and are moving towards a common
destiny. It is, for example, now almost universally accepted
that in the nuclear age the whole world is the smallest possible
unit of survival.

The United Nations Organisation is open to every con-
ceivable form of criticism, yet it is the great prophetic fact
of our day—prophetic, in the sense that it points beyond
itself to a true world community, to a time when its present
gossamer web of international obligation, which can be
snapped with contemptuous ease, will have been superseded
by a strong and durable structure of ethics and law. But we
cannot fold our arms and wait for that day. Those who
believe that mankind is truly one and that this is where
their primary allegiance lies must think and behave as citizens of the world. Southern Africa does not float in a vacuum.
It is joined to the rest of the world by a thousand filaments.
The Rhodesian immigration authorities can keep out un-

desirable persons but they cannot keep out undesirable ideas. The power and spirit of our age expressed in such ways as a growing abhorrence of all forms of discrimination cannot be resisted indefinitely by ideological barriers or apartheid laws or phoney declarations of independence.

When I am asked what Christians in Europe and the United States, who have no access to the corridors of power, can do to help their brethren in Southern Africa other than all the paraphernalia of boycott, sanction and demonstration which seems so laughably inadequate, I would say that such gestures form part of the moral pressure which the whole of mankind can bring to bear upon any one part of it. One world; one humanity; therefore, one battle-line. Every blow, every pathetic blow struck for racial equality and human dignity in Wolverhampton or Cambridge reverberates in Salisbury or Pretoria; every erosion of justice in Westminster, Washington, Moscow or Peking slams shut a prison-cell door in Southern Africa. In the day of small things, the efforts of small men achieve a significance which would be denied them in the day of grand strategies that demand men of heroic proportions to work the levers of power.

So count me among the prisoners of hope, not because I have any clear idea at this minute where the road to justice and equality in Southern Africa lies: I haven't. But I refuse to believe that the forward advance of all mankind will be held up by any group of people who try to hold a part of it in thrall. I may believe that history is mysterious but I don't believe it's meaningless. And I believe in hope not so much in terms of resolution as in terms of resurrection, through seeds growing secretly and leaven transforming whole lumps. And it's not a humanist vision I've been putting across. For me Christ holds the key to the door of the cell in which the prisoners of hope work and pray and struggle to make what could be must be.

THE CHRISTIAN LIFE

CHAPTER SEVENTEEN

BORN OF A WOMAN

by Professor C. F. D. MOULE, Lady Margaret Professor of Divinity

There can be few more poignant scenes in the whole Gospel story than when the mother of Jesus and his brothers tried to rescue Jesus from what they believed to be a mad career. The family of Jesus, to quote from St. Mark in the N.E.B., 'set out to take charge of him; for people were saying that he was out of his mind'. But when they reach the house where Jesus is preaching there is such a dense crowd both inside the house and round the door that they can't get at him. So they send in a message asking him to come out to them. But all Jesus does is to say, 'Who is my mother? Who are my brothers?' And looking round at those who were sitting in the circle about him he said, 'Here are my mother and my brothers. Whoever does the will of God is my brother, my sister, my mother.'

We can imagine the circumstances. It's easy to understand how the family of Jesus would watch him and shake their heads. They would say, perhaps, that popular preaching is no career for a loyal Jew to adopt. Jesus, of course, commands immense audiences, but where is it going to lead anybody? His success has gone to his head. Yes, and his success may well cost him his head. Remember John the Baptist. It's all very well to be popular as a freelance evangelist, but this is no way to earn one's living. One suspects that the brothers of Jesus and perhaps his sisters said this kind of thing about him with a touch of jealousy in their hearts; jealousy for the brother whose superb intellect and magnetic personality had established a natural ascendancy over them. One imagines his mother also, perhaps, saying this kind of thing but without jealousy—only with agonising apprehension. And now in the scene with which we began it has come to a head-on collision. She and the rest of her

family have been sent to rescue him, as they imagine, from
a disastrous course; but Jesus will not even come out to
parley with them. 'My family,' he says, 'are those who obey
God.' It was a calculated rebuff, and it must have gone
through Mary's heart like a knife; and indeed that is exactly
why I began with that scene from St. Mark, because I think
it helps to illuminate the oracular words to which we listened
in the second lesson from St. Luke about Mary being pierced
to the heart with a sword.

This is the story of the occasion which we celebrate today,
the Feast of the Presentation of Christ in the Temple. It's
often and popularly called the Feast of the Purification
because the Mosaic code, represented here by the Book of
Leviticus, regarded childbirth as something which rendered
the mother ritually unclean and prescribed purificatory rights.
It was these that the mother of Jesus had come up to the
Temple to perform. But, thanks to the teaching of our Lord
himself, we as Christians know that there is nothing impure
about childbirth; and properly speaking the Christian festival should always be known as the Festival of the Presentation of Christ in the Temple—the other purpose for which
Mary had also come up to Jerusalem: to present to God
her first-born son. This too was a Mosaic prescription according to the Book of Exodus. The origin of this ritual may
for all we know go right back to the myths of pre-history,
perhaps to the savage days of human sacrifice. But the
Hebrew religious genius had taken it and refined it and made
it into a beautiful sacrament in which the first male child was
acknowledged as belonging to God and was only bought
back, as it were redeemed, by an offering to God from the
parents. And so Mary and Joseph offered the sacrifice and
performed the ritual both for purification and for presentation; and then there came upon the scene the saintly old
man Simeon, and he uttered his moving little farewell to
life: 'Now at last I can die happy because I have seen with
my own eyes what I have waited all my life to see.' But you'll
remember that Simeon added to his Nunc Dimittis that dark
oracle. 'This child,' he said, 'is destined to be a sign which
men reject, and you too', turning to Mary, 'you too shall be
pierced to the heart. Many in Israel will stand or fall because
of him, and thus the secret thoughts of many will be laid
bare.'

What did Simeon mean? He appears to have meant that the little child lying in his arms is going to be a bringer of crisis, a divider. In his presence men will be forced to take sides. He will be either like a stone in their path over which they trip and fall, or else like that other stone, a firm foundation stone, on which they can stand upright or build to last; one or the other. And men are going to resent being forced to this decision and men will oppose it. Yes, and Mary herself, says Simeon, will also be divided within herself. She will be pierced to the heart with a sword. How could our Lord's mother know what that meant? But she had to learn, and the hard lesson began all too soon. It is St. Luke again who tells us that other story of the twelve-year-old Jesus going up with his parents to the festival in Jerusalem and, unknown to them, staying on behind and giving his parents three days of intense anxiety and at the end, when at last he was discovered, saying, almost casually, 'But surely you knew I must be in my Father's house?' What a premonition for Mary, a touch of Simeon's sword! And now, in the scene with which we began, here is the open rift. Christian piety and devotion, naturally and rightly, have concentrated, when thinking of the mother of our Lord, on the purity and the depth of one who could have such a son. But we don't add to our understanding of her depth by refusing to allow that she had to reach it and learn it the hard way.

We need not, perhaps we ought not, to refuse to contemplate her painful experiences. In a word, if we are going to be realistic, what we are witnessing in these stories is mother and son experiencing what we have learnt to call the 'generation gap'. What son could have been more precious to his mother than this son to such a mother? The temptation to try to keep him for herself must have been exceptionally strong. And again what son can have run ahead of his mother further and more quickly than Jesus? In our natural reverence for his mother we easily forget that, if the Christian faith is right in believing that Jesus had a unique relationship with God, then even the best of mothers must early have been out-distanced in spiritual depth and vision by her son. She must have been puzzled, she must have been left standing.

So here are all the ingredients for a uniquely painful rift between the two generations and for an exceptionally frustrating breakdown in communication. I owe it to a paper by your own Vicar read in Westminster College that there has been borne home on me especially clearly of late the friction that I do not think we can escape if we read the records honestly. But there are two redeeming factors that saved the pain from becoming bitter and that turned the tragedy into something creative. One is the steadily godward attitude of the mother, the other is the extreme tenderness of the son, despite his resolute will. And these are factors which I think it is worth our pondering because they still operate for us. Not that we know very much about that family and their relationships—pious imagination has run riot in its lust to know more than can be known, and the legends outside the canonical scriptures are seldom edifying.

But for the matter in hand, it is enough if we may believe that the family of Jesus was a godly family and that the mother of Jesus remained faithful even through the harshnesses, and if we may believe, too, in a supreme tenderness in the character of Jesus combined with his quiet firmness. Take the first of these, the godly family. The ritual of the presentation of the first-born son was a formal recognition that he belonged to God and that if he belonged to the parents it was only by divine permission. In the case of Hannah, whose story we heard in the first lesson, the child was not redeemed. He was actually given away. Hannah brought her little son Samuel to the sanctuary of Shilo to leave him there as a minister. She surrendered him. But with most Jewish parents (and our Lord's mother was no exception) it was rather like a sacrament of dedication, a ritualised acknowledgment of God's sovereign rights as the begetter and possessor of all his people.

And I dare to suggest that it was this clear acknowledgment of God, expressed and focused in a specific ritual—something that could be dated and placed, for example, on February the First in the Temple at Jerusalem—that helped Mary to endure and to remain faithful amid all the tensions of the 'generation gap'. Even though again and again she may have longed to possess and hold her beloved son, even though she had the agony of watching him grow away from her—an agony like a sword in herself—she knew nevertheless that she had given him to the Lord. Had she not clinched this obedience by the sacrifice and by the ritual on that unforgettable day? How could she waver in her determination to treat Jesus as really belonging to the Lord? And so she endured. Though he may even have seemed to rebuff her she stuck with him. At any rate we find her with the disciples at the beginning of the story of the Acts, and if the picture in St. John's Gospel is true, at least in spirit, she was with him at his end. Her religion and her sacramental focusing of her fixed intention towards God held her firm in times of stress. And that can be true of us. It is the dedicated—those who, among God's other worshipping people, have sealed their loyalty with serious intention—who are held through days of difficulty. The sacramental moments—baptism, confirmation, Holy Communion, marriage—these are not just empty forms, but are invaluable anchorages that hold a life and help to make its loyalty firm, solid and objective in all the storms that try to shake it. A steady, godward attitude stressed in worship and in sacrament may rescue a threatened relationship.

The other supreme factor is the son's absolute tenderness. I suppose that one of the hardest things that a son or daughter may have to do is to be firm with the parent. Sooner or later the young person has to stand on his own feet; he has to make his own decisions even if they are totally wrong; he has to take responsibility for himself. Then a parent who possessively tries to interfere ought to be firmly handled. But—this is the whole point—there is no excuse for harsh, insensitive handling of the situation. Firmness can, and should, be combined with the most sensitive gentleness, with an intuitive, imaginative understanding of the parent's feelings, with a warmth of affection that never gives up even when there is misunderstanding, with a yearning for a full, tender relationship. This emerges in the traditions about Jesus, at any rate in St. John's Gospel. He rebukes his mother when she interferes at Cana just as, in the Synoptic story, he sends his message to those who come to rescue him. But at the climax, in the intolerable pain upon the cross, he still thinks of his mother by tenderly committing her to his closest friend. Jesus has combined unremittingly firm adherence to duty with the utmost tenderness and imaginative considerateness.

When there is godliness like this on both sides of the gap, then there is always hope. There is hope too when there is real devotion given only on one side—junior or senior. What cannot children do for their parents by combining firmness with tenderness, a firmness and a tenderness springing from a real dedication to the Lord? And what cannot a parent do who remains always the same—openhearted, tender, tenacious in love, always welcoming, even when refusing to hold on to the child or coerce him? Without religion (acknowledged or unacknowledged) on either side, it is hard to see how this disastrous situation can be really successful met. However, there are always Christian friends who watch and pray. So all of us who thank God today for the patience and dedication of the mother of our Lord, and for our Lord's own perfect response to his heavenly Father's will, in this and in all things, must often pray and offer our active obedience for the healing of such troubles and for the constructive bridging of the 'generation gap'. This is a festival of parenthood and sonship; and in it we offer now our active eagerness to be used by God in making right this relationship.

CHAPTER EIGHTEEN

IN HOSPITAL

by the Reverend MICHAEL PATON, formerly Chaplain of
United Sheffield Hospitals, Vicar of St. Mark, Sheffield

Hospitals vary a good deal. Those I serve are a group—
two acute hospitals, one for women, one for children, and
various annexes and clinics. The acute hospitals have the
usual standbys of hospitals, hearts, strokes, cancer, accidents;
the accidents in Sheffield are perhaps rather different from
the accidents here. There are the usual motor-vehicle accidents, there are rock-climbing accidents, there are mining
and steel accidents, people whose arms or legs have been
crushed or burnt by hot or cold steel, or by falls of rock,
or by trains underground in the mines going over their feet.
You shake hands with a miner who's just had his leg crushed
and you find he is already missing a couple of fingers. Many
of the patients lead hard and disagreeable lives in many ways
in their work. The women's hospital is a straightforward
women's hospital with a mixture of babies, with all the joy,
and of course sometimes in the case of some people distress,
of new birth, and gynaecological termination of pregnancy
—that is, abortions. The children's hospital covers all sorts
of things, again the usual things that children get wrong
with them like very bad burns; a child puts a firework in a
very old tin which he sees about and it happens to be full
of petrol vapour and the child gets seventy per cent burns
and six weeks later dies. We have a great many children
suffering from a condition known as *spina bifida*, which is
a malformation of the spinal chord usually appearing in the
back. This used to mean you had a condition of water on the
head (*hydrocephalous*) and probably fairly soon died. There
is now an operation done which makes it possible to recover
a varying amount of use, in some cases extremely good, in
other cases not so good. Babies come from a very wide radius,
in some cases hundreds of miles away, to the hospital to
have these operations. This means a great many emergency

baptisms. And there are also the problems for the staff raised by medical techniques of transplant and resuscitation and the relief of pain—and these are problems which are being raised for the future by techniques now. There are about 1,500 beds, there are about 40,000 admissions every year— the average stay is about ten to twelve days.

Those patients who come in all sorts of ways have all, I think, without exception got fears. We all have them, but when you get that note or the phone call saying, 'Will you please come in tomorrow?' the fears rise to the surface. There's the fear of pain, the ordinary straightforward fear that any child who hears about hospital feels that 'they will hurt me'. There is the fear of publicity. If you happen not to have lived in a barrack room or a dormitory or some sort of public situation like that, it's extremely disagreeable to think—as people do think—that they will have to dress and undress and be examined and so on in public. In fact, of course, both these fears are not usually very badly realised. Pain-killing techniques are very good and the publicity is not so bad because there are curtains around each bed. There is the fear of the family upset. How will Grannie manage? What will my wife do? What about the children? There is the disruption of plans. I was going to go on holiday in June, but shall I be ready in time? There is the fear of the unknown, and there is the fear of death. These fears really come down to the two concerns of human life—the people we love and our parting from them, and secondly, my own capacity and its decay. As for those fears, some of them may be realised, some of them not—we don't know which.

Those 1,500 beds are the *raison d'être* for the staff, of whom there is a payroll of about 4,000. But yet this collection of patients also provides for the staff a career (or rather many different careers), a vocation, very worrying responsibilities, decisions to be made that most of us would hate to have to make, and made in a hurry. There is the heartache. The staff themselves are under much strain. The nearer they are to the patient the more the strain. A girl of eighteen begins nursing and she is faced quite soon with the problem of how she is to cope with the distress that she is faced with. Is she to become involved? If she is crying her eyes out in the sluice every day, she won't be a very good nurse. Or is she to become detached? There are examples I presume in every hospital of people who have become so detached that they are lacquered over, you can't get at them, least of all the patients can't get at them. That's not the way. So they try to become neither one thing nor the other, but to remain human but also efficient. This is a tremendous strain; and this is one of the reasons for the apparent crudity of medical jokes and medical conversation. It's a kind of means whereby the profession among themselves may relieve these anxieties and the tremendous tension that they have.

A hospital is not really like an ant heap, because there are conflicting desires and conflicting aims; and the Christian presence is the presence of Christ. It's shown, it seems to me, by the neuro-surgeon (he didn't tell me but his wife did) who had made a rule that he would never if possible break bad news to a patient if the patient was lying flat on his back. Get them set up against a pillow and they can take it better if you're looking at them and they are not horizontal. That is just one instance among many others of thoughtfulness of that kind. It is shown too by the medical student who when talking to the mother of an abnormal child who had died— a very greatly abnormal child—was asking her what she was going to call it and so on, and was talking to her in a human way. He left her and joined his fellow medical students and they said, 'What were you doing?' and he said, 'I was just talking to her about her child, and she was telling me what she was going to call it.' And they said, 'What was she going to call it, Boris Karloff?' I now see that that crude reference to Frankenstein's monster, which seemed so heartless when I first heard it, was just another way of reacting to that woman's trouble. Well, it seemed to me that that medical student was showing Christ.

Sometimes things are quite inexplicable. No one knows exactly what is happening or how it happens. But that something strange and marvellous happens seems to be clear. I was asked to go to see a woman by three different people— a nurse on the ward, the ward sister and another patient. They said she was bitter. She had been involved in a motor accident with her fairly young, married daughter. They were both in the same part of the ward in almost adjoining beds. I went to see her fairly late on a Sunday night, about nine o'clock, when the ward was beginning to settle down and it was fairly quiet. We had a conversation and she told me how bitter she felt because her husband had died about six months before. He had died from one of 'the shocks which we are heir to'. We talked and I gave her a blessing, said an evening prayer with her, and she seemed quite settled, composed and serene in a way; I had a word with her daughter, who said how grateful she was to me for coming to see her mother. I left them about half past nine. At three o'clock the next morning the daughter had a pulmonary embolism and died. I was told the next morning, and went to see her mother who had been moved to another bed. When I came to her, she looked at me with an expression of misery, bitterness and despair, and said, 'I wouldn't have your job.' She was there for another eight weeks, and I saw her from time to time. When she was discharged, she seemed to me to be a transformed person. Before, she was unbelievably bitter—saying that if she could get the young man who had caused that accident hung, she would do so, and she had said this to his mother who had come to see her in hospital. But when she left, though she was very far from the conventional church person, she was saying things like, 'Well, good seems to have come out of it.' I think she had said that because good had come out of it, and for no other reason. Why was this? Well, I don't think myself it was a coincidence that the sister of that ward was a remarkably humorous, understanding and committed Christian. How God works—how he used what we were all trying to do with that woman for whom many prayers were said and for her daughter and for her son-in-law—no one knows. But that something happened to her while she was in hospital seemed clear to me.

The chaplain has his place, but no one knows what it is. The chaplain is not a Christ-like person any more than any of us are, and yet, there as a Christian, he is to be like Christ and may be used like Christ as target and peacemaker—you never know when it's going to be. I called on a man who, after a slight fencing in the conversation, said he had a coronary and was terrified of having another. Naturally when a thing has happened once, it is more likely that it will happen again than if you had never had it. We went on talking and eventually he came out with two things. First of all that he didn't believe that, if he did have a fatal coronary, there was anything for him beyond that. He had no belief in any kind of resurrection. Secondly, that the reason he didn't believe this was that his daughter had died at the age of nineteen, and the bitterness that he felt about God's failure (as he saw it) to rescue his daughter had been with him all that time since them. Or you may go to see other people when they have just had their pre-medical before an operation, so that they shouldn't be roused or talked to for a long time. So you say perhaps, 'Well, I'll just give you a blessing for your operation,' and they say, sometimes, in the most heartfelt way, 'If you would,' and you just give them a blessing with a hand on their forehead with the old words that have been used for so many hundreds of years, and they are at peace. Then six months later they will stop you in the street and say how much it meant to them. How much did you know though, the chaplain, of what was going on? Any Christian does just what he or she can and the Lord seems to be there. The way patients help each other is equally strange and encouraging.

It seems to me that what Christ does in all this is that, first of all, he shows us by people direct, or by words we happen to hear or read, that the flesh matters. After all, Bethlehem stands for the Word made flesh. People who are in fleshly trouble, and who have perhaps assumed that this incredibly, complex and complicated mass that we call a body will work well, may feel all kinds of things when it stops working well—they may feel ashamed, they may feel disgusted and they may feel in despair; but flesh matters. If our Lord was content to wear flesh, then so can we be.

Secondly, Christ takes suffering seriously. In a hospital we are, sometimes at any rate, going to have (and certainly be faced with, in other people), suffering. Christ is crucified. Though we don't understand precisely what was happening on that cross, we can know that here is man suffering in obedience. So when we are faced with our own decay, when we are faced with our own apparent desolation, when we are faced with publicity and parting, we are close to Christ. Christ has entered into these things that happen to us. One theologian has said 'These things really count for atheism if you take them straight, but God has dealt with this somehow, for he has entered into these things and shown that they can count for him.'

And thirdly, Christ gives us our bearings through his presence. If the resurrection is true, then we are forced to ask, 'What is it true for? Have I got to wait until I'm dead before the resurrection means anything to me?' Surely not! It makes a difference to the bearing, the orientation and the direction of our life now. In hospital, above all, we ask ourselves, 'What am I, when I am stripped of my degrees, of my handsomeness, of my memory, of my job, of my clothes and, in the end, of my life? What am I? Where am I going? And what am I when I have all these things? Is there any difference?' 'No,' says Christ, surely, 'there is no difference. You are a child of God. You are made for joy.'

CHAPTER NINETEEN

PRAYING

by Canon STEPHEN VERNEY,
formerly of Coventry Cathedral

People are becoming hungry and thirsty for prayer. You can feel the change. We are becoming hungry and thirsty for the real experience, in our own hearts, of the peace and the power of God.

May I tell you a story which I heard from Archbishop Bloom? He told us that a lady once came to him and said, 'Can you teach me to pray? I have said prayers all my life, but I have never experienced God.' So he said to her, 'Go home and tidy your room and sit comfortably in your armchair for a quarter of an hour, and whatever you do don't pray.' So she went home, she tidied her room, she sat in her armchair. And now for the first time in years she found herself looking at the room, and noticing with pleasure its various architectural shapes and the colours of the furnishings. She heard the ticking of the clock; tick-tock went the clock, and the silence grew so profound that she felt herself slipping into prayer. But she knew that this was the one thing she wasn't allowed to do. So she took out her knitting, and what with the tick-tock of the clock and the click of the needles the silence grew even more profound, and she became aware, at the heart of the silence, of a Presence.

Here is another story that I heard recently from a sixteen-year-old girl. Her boy friend at school was very depressed and she went for a walk with him into a field. They sat on the ground in silence and she tried very hard to will peace into his heart. Then she began to understand that she couldn't force peace into him, so she relaxed and became aware of the peace all around them and then the peace came through her and filled her boy friend's heart. After a while they returned to school and she went to the library to read, and her eyes were opened and she saw the heat rising out of the radiators, and that all the books on the shelves were laughing.

So we learn the fundamental secret of prayer. Prayer is not us trying to grab hold of God. Prayer is to recognise God coming to us. This is called contemplation, and is what Jesus taught. 'Consider the flowers of the field,' he said. Open the eyes in your head and look at them, and as you look, open the eyes of your spirit and see, within the flowers, God. See God's artistry so that Solomon in all his splendour was not attired like one of these. Consider the birds of the air, and as you look at them see God's generosity feeding them.

See God everywhere, recognise his presence at the heart of all things. Through all things he is revealing his character. Heaven and earth are full of his glory. Through all things. God is coming to you, giving you himself, claiming your co-operation in his purpose. The more accurately you look the more clearly you will recognise God and discover his purpose. Look with the microscope at the living cell, you will see a marvel of ordered complexity. Look with the insight of the biologist at the whole process of evolution from the primitive cell. You will see the process stretching over hundreds of millions of years which is a growth in the same ordered complexity, a process which seems to flow like a river towards the goal where all things shall belong to each other, all things embrace each other in one perfect complexity, each thing being fully itself, and all together making one harmony, one music, one unity of love.

Recognise God coming to us. This is the heart of prayer, of contemplation. But I would want to add: recognise God coming to us through the here and now. God is pressing towards us through all things, at all times and in all places which are for us the here and the now. This includes not only things, times and places which seem to us beautiful and good but also those which seem ugly and bad.

One of the great evils of today is pollution. When we consider the flowers and the birds, in the here and now of 1970, we see man destroying them with chemicals. But your Vicar has been telling me that his researches into pollution have brought him, with a new sense of reality, face to face with God. My own researches, over the last six years, have been into cities, and two years ago I went to Calcutta and visited some of those slums where people live in conditions not fit for animals. Human excreta oozes out of their rickety houses and fouls the paths between them. Here is the problem of the city at its most terrible. Here are people, the chief planner told me, who live beyond the threshold of hope. But when I got there and tried to take photographs of the squalor I couldn't, because I was surrounded by crowds of laughing children. A proud, upstanding Indian lady welcomed me into her home, where three generations were living together with human warmth and dignity. This was more shocking to me than the poverty. Here at the heart of the world's urban problem I found the spirit of man springing up triumphant out of the quagmire of his own excreta. And at that point I encountered God.

Or two days ago—because one must speak of the here and now if one is really to encounter God—two days ago I was walking through London with an ex-junkie who has recently come off heroin. My eyes were opened to see all around us a different world. People with shaggy hair and dressed in rags and dangles smiled at him, though they had never seen him before, as being members together of a secret fraternity. One dreamy figure got up from a seat in the park and told us that he was just off cycling into France to visit a commune. Another, with an old blanket stuck over his head as a poncho, told us how he had been watching twelve little ducklings take to the water for the first time. My friend, having recently come off heroin, knows that what gets you hooked is not the drug itself, but the experience of peace which passes all understanding, the experience of being 'turned on', the camaraderie. So he is setting up a trust to open a centre where people may come to experience the reality of these things, not the shadow of them which is induced by heroin. What is this extraordinary happening? An ex-addict standing by his friends and encouraging them to be free? Peace which passes all understanding? People turned on? Camaraderie? Open your eyes and within the here and now of the drug problem you will encounter God.

I say encounter, and not just recognise, because the God whom you recognise is always the God who is also claiming you to co-operate with him. When Isaiah knew that heaven and earth were full of God's glory, he also heard a voice saying, 'Whom shall I send? Who will go for me?' So we must add one more clause to our description of contempla-

tive prayer: to recognise God coming to us through the
here and now and to co-operate with him. Contemplation
is to open our whole personality to God so that he can take
possession of our emotions, our thinking and our will. It's
not us grabbing hold of God, it's God laying hold of us.
And Christian contemplation is to be turned on by Christ
(the Hero-in us), so that the spirit of God's creative power
can flow through us.

This brings us to the very heart of prayer, and to the
absolute here and now where we encounter God face to
face. The absolute here and now for me is myself. I have to
open to God the very centre of my own being. I am afraid
to do this because I feel within myself dark and powerful
forces, which toss me to and fro, and which I prefer to keep
clamped down in the hold of my subconscious. I feel my
sexuality, my aggression, my fear, my greed. Surely this is
no place, at the centre of myself, to come face to face with
God? Yet this is exactly what Jesus taught. He promises in
passionate words that if we will have the courage to stand
with him and to open ourselves before God, then out of the
very centre of ourselves will flow the river of God's Spirit.
'Come to me,' he cries, 'he that believes in me out of his
belly shall flow rivers of living water.' Out of the very centre
of his instincts, his emotions, out of his belly, out of his
guts, out of his sex, his aggression, his fear, his greed, shall
spring up the power and the peace of God.

The heart of contemplative prayer is to experience that
truth in times which are specially set apart for this encounter
with God. Gradually we may come to see him at all times
and in all places, as we are shopping, eating, talking to our
friends. But until we become very experienced in prayer
and sensitive to his presence, we need special times in which
we can encounter God—the silence at the centre of ourselves. We have to go beyond words, beyond thoughts or
feelings about God, beyond pictures of him, and to plunge
into that silence where HE IS. The approach to this silence
may well be through relaxation of the body—to sit comfortably, attentive, expectant. 'Behold,' he says, 'I stand at
the door and knock. If any man hear my voice and open the
door, I will come in.'

Perhaps the best preparation for his coming is to repeat
his name. This prayer of the name is used in the East, in

Hindu and Buddhist spirituality. It consists of repeating again and again the name of God, or beyond the name of God the syllable OM, which expresses the mystery of his presence. And as you repeat this sound, so your mind concentrates and grows still and you become aware of the secret depths of joy and peace where God dwells in your heart. For the Russian or Greek Orthodox Christian, the prayer has consisted in saying again and again the name of Jesus, or in a somewhat longer form, 'Jesus have mercy upon me.' I once asked a Greek monk to describe the prayer to me and he told me that he prayed it chiefly in the silent hours of the night. 'When I begin,' he said, 'it is ME and HIM. Then it becomes HIM and ME. Then it becomes only HIM.' Through the silence, through the here and now of yourself, as you really are, God comes, and you become Christ. God says to you, 'You are my beloved Son,' and he calls you by your secret name which is known only to himself, and you reply, 'Abba, Father.' Such is the heart of private contemplation, from which flows the river of the power of God.

But there is a kind of prayer of the name that may be even more real. 'When two or three are gathered together in my name, there am I among them.'

During the last few weeks I have been meeting every Wednesday each week with a group of eight people who are trying to discover how to be the Church in the urban world, to celebrate the Eucharist in each others' houses and to eat and to talk together. As we have grown together, the Eucharist, the meal and the conversation have gradually flowed together into one single action. We use the rhythm of an ordinary evening when friends meet together for supper. We exchange our news for a time, and then sit at the table to enjoy the food and the wine. When the cheese and fruit and coffee are on the table one of us reads the Gospel, and then in that marvellous moment of human intimacy, when a company of people have eaten together, we discuss the Gospel for an hour. The discussion passes naturally into prayer. We all pray extempore, about any concerns of the moment. Prayer passes naturally into penitence. We sit for a time in silence and know the forgiveness of God. Then one of us declares God's peace and we hug each other and express our friendship in any way which is appropriate. Then the host breaks bread and takes the cup in his hands.

When I did this for the first time a few weeks ago my eyes
were opened, and I recognised God, coming to us through
the here and now, and claiming our co-operation in his great
purpose. I found myself saying, 'Likewise after supper he
took the cup.'

Yes, of course, after supper. In that most natural and
human moment in the here and now of your friendship, and
of your intention to advance my Kingdom, as you are
gathered together in my name, 'there am I among you'.

CHAPTER TWENTY

WITNESS, PROTEST, DISCIPLESHIP

by Canon ERIC JAMES,
Precentor of Southwark Cathedral

I want to speak to you this morning on 'Protest'. To Milton and to Shakespeare to protest meant to proclaim, to affirm, to vow, to witness. I believe that this linguistic connection should never entirely be severed. 'Seeing we are compassed about with so great a cloud of witnesses; the Greek word there for witness is very much akin to our word martyr. Martyrs, witnesses, proclaimers, protesters, they all have, should have, much in common.

And there really is my first point: that protest for the Christian is fundamentally positive, not negative. It is always fundamentally affirmation at cost, at risk, grounded in the great and central truths of the Christian faith, that all men are equally valuable in the sight of God; equally loved by him, be they Vietnamese, Viet Cong, Russian, Chinese, American, British, white Rhodesian, black Rhodesian, Israeli, Egyptian. In his love God created us all. In his love he was made man. In his love he revealed in his life and death and triumphant suffering the nature and destiny of man, the nature of that love which is the origin, sustenance, completion and goal of all men.

The motive of protest for the Christian is always grounded in him whose nature and whose name is love.

And I believe it is wholly right that if, for instance, smaller nations like Czechoslovakia become pawns in the hands of the great powers, fodder in the military machine, as Christians we should struggle to think how we can demonstrate most powerfully what we want to affirm in such a situation. We may not be able to do a thing, but that does not relieve us of trying to do what we can. But what about the method of protest for the Christian?

The method, the weapon of Christian protest must always be the method of love, and often, indeed, of violent love.

I find myself asked quite often these days, 'Is violence ever justified?' Personally I have no doubt that it is. I believe it does despite to the truth to suggest that Christ's love lacked violence and aggression. If human beings are involved in loving, aggression will be involved. Christ would not have been human had he had no aggression. But the question is not so much 'Is violence justified?' as 'What kind of violence and aggression is justified?' The Christian can never separate violence from his reflection on the nature of love.

Archbishop William Temple once described a pacifist as someone who loves his enemies and hates his friends. Indeed, I heard him once during the Second World War put the question, 'Which is more loving—to kill two million Germans in order to save ten million Jews, or to keep your powder dry?' His question was not uttered glibly. He was pointing out that in this world human choices are usually the lesser of two evils. The man who thinks he has clean hands and a pure heart because he has not taken up arms may be a self-deceiving idealist who has not taken seriously enough the permanent and inescapable relation between love and power. You do not by refusing to wield power escape your responsibility for wielding it. And often those who oppose the use of violence ignore the violence that is already there in the situation, suppressing justice and making what is at first sight 'Law and Order' simply the maintenance by force of an established disorder and injustice. The established disorder in Hitler's Germany, in South Africa and Greece and South America and Northern Ireland and many another place today, often parade as law and order. But let it be said that the Christian has at every stage to weigh the effects of his methods of protest in the balance of love. He has to ask again and again: What is the most loving thing to be done at this moment? And there is no cheap and easy method of computation, no method that will guarantee that we have the right answer. But, as I say, the Christian has to weigh the effects of his actions at every stage in the balance of love.

At this moment it may be wrong to take up arms. Now there is still time for negotiation. Now there is still time for some creative act of reconciliation, or of trust and faith, that will make all the difference. But how can you be certain that the creative act of trust will not be taken as, and in fact will not be, the fatal act of weakness? You cannot be certain. That is the definition of an act of faith. There is never an act of faith without risk. But the question is: is it loving to risk so much? Too much risk, if you're risking someone else's survival, can be as unloving as too little. In the present situation of Vietnam, for instance, one thing is clear: we are not in a situation, and never have been, in which there is only one way left: violence. Neither are we in a situation in which the Vietnamese are all right and the Viet Cong all wrong. We are in a situation in which whatever negotiations there can be should be, and in which some acts of trust and faith must be made. I remember a year or so ago when we had the great 'demo' in London, saying to myself that if demonstrating to that end in, say, Britain, will have some effect towards this end; if (and this is no certainty), then let us demonstrate. And if that demonstration causes some scuffles, some violence, some damage, let us say to ourselves, 'Better some violence and damage here than interminable violence and indescribable damage there in the Far East'. But let us all be clear: we cannot be saints today and be unconcerned about witnessing to the need for love to be brought to bear upon the grim realities of the war in Vietnam. It has been my lot to travel to the U.S.A. almost each year for the last five years and of one thing I am certain: the American Government wouldn't have made the moves towards negotiations that it has were it not for the volume of public protest from ordinary men and women.

At this point as we try to shape our Christian mind on 'protest' I want to direct your minds to the supreme act of witness of Christ himself: his death upon the cross, which down the ages has been the inspiration of countless saints, and martyrs, and witnesses. It has to be said that characteristically, supremely, Christ in his life and death chose the way not of suffering inflicted upon others, but upon himself; not masochistically, not for its own sake, not for his own sake, but for others. We have to study, reflect upon, consider again and again Christ's life and death in relation to this profound mystery of reconciliation between man and man, and race and race, and nation and nation. Consider Christ's methods of protest in the cleansing of the Temple. The motive and the method of protest for the Christian have always to be seen within the context of love, Christ's reconciling love. And that may have quite a lot to say about the way we behave on protest marches, and upon, indeed, the creative act of faith required to move the log-jam between negotiators in such a situation as that now existing in the negotiations over Vietnam.

Motive: method—and I want to add another 'M' now to these thoughts on protest—moment. Jesus was always talking about his 'hour'. 'Mine hour is not yet come.' I think the choice of the right moment to protest is always very important indeed. At the height of Nazi power, when the great Christian martyr Dietrich Bonhoeffer and his friend Eberhard Bethge were attending a public function at which there was much praise for the Nazis, and many Nazi salutes, at one point Bethge saw to his horror that Bonhoeffer was saluting, and with apparent vigour. When Bethge showed distress, Bonhoeffer replied, 'Put up your arm! This thing isn't worth dying for!' A few years later Bonhoeffer was dead; martyred. When do you make your protest—on Vietnam—or on, say, the race relations situation? This could be a matter of vocation, indeed, of temperament. Paul Schneider, the first martyr of the Confessional Church in Germany, instinctively resisted. While Bonhoeffer was giving his students a clearly worked-out training which would enable them to meet the problems of their day and not be out-thought by the so-called German Christians, several groups of ministers were reading their Bibles faithfully, confident that these gave them clear, undeniable directions. Bonhoeffer respected these men, but he saw that someone had to work out the complex implications of obedience. Paul Schneider died without getting much further than a single-minded recognition that he must obey God rather than man. He thought, lived, witnessed and died in a way that reads like the Acts of the Apostles. Such men were needed; are needed. Bonhoeffer had another task, which while it risked martyrdom did not require it immediately. His hour had not yet come.

Four years ago I went to South Africa for a couple of months to preach in various places. I spoke my mind, but I did not want to provoke my deportation without having had a chance to say a thing. (It would have been such a waste of a good fare.) Besides, there is always a very great deal to learn at first hand that can radically change what you have to say.

But not having been intentionally provocative, rather the reverse, I remember the bishop of one of the first dioceses I preached in coming up to me after my first sermon in his cathedral. 'Eric,' he said, 'I don't want to stop you saying anything you feel in conscience you must say. But may I say that if you say tomorrow night in the cathedral what you have said tonight, Mrs. X will probably withdraw her pledge, which is one of the largest annual contributions to the diocese; and there are others like her. And if they do it will be the African clergy who are bound to suffer most. They can't move elsewhere. They have no other means of employment. It's their pay you'll be stopping.' Well, I think in fact the African clergy would gladly have suffered for my proclamation of our Gospel, but I have never personally had a clearer reminder of the complexity of witness, of protest. The witness would have cost me little, but others a lot. It's not difficult to understand when you go to South Africa the reasoning of some priests who say, 'If I am always protesting I shall be deported, and I shall deprive the African Church of another minister. And which is worse: an African church deprived of the presence of a minister, or an African church with ministers present deprived of the voice of protest? I believe that the Church in South African probably needs each generation an Ambrose Reeves, a Trevor Huddleston, a Bishop Edward Crowther; but it probably needs also those who, as the Psalmist says, 'keep silence, yea, even from good words' though it is pain and grief to them.

Motive: method: moment. But there's one other factor that I would like to mention which I've already hinted at, and I think it should be particularly part of Christian protest so I emphasise it. The awareness of the complexity of a situation is not always particularly great amongst Christians. People talk rather too easily, too glibly, of the Christian attitude, and the Christian way, even of the Christian answer. William Blake said, 'He who would do good to another must do it in minute particulars.' It is probably a sign of old age that I am a wee bit worried by the degree of irresponsibility that there has been in some of the student protest in recent months; indeed, the avowed anarchy. He who would love another must do it in minute particulars, in down-to-earth details of motive and method and moment and even more than that. There is luxury about the cry of protest, the mere words of protest. There is luxury even about a protest march. You must not only walk to gain your objectives. You must walk with them when you have gained them. You must learn to wield power, power in subordination to love. Christian political action is the wielding of power in subordination to love, subordinate not in a general sort of way but in minute particulars. I always want to say to students who are protesting, 'You want power? By God you shall have it. But don't drop it. And don't tire when you realise it involves minute particulars.'

I have in fact a favourite text, which I think is relevant at this point: 'In the fifteenth year of the reign of Tiberius Caesar, Pontius Pilate being governor of Judea, and Herod being tetrarch of Galilee, and his brother Philip tetrarch of the region of Iturea and Trachonitis, and Lysanias tetrarch of Abilene, in the high priesthood of Annas and Caiaphas, the Word of God came to John.' I like that text because I doubt whether you could ever gather together in one verse a bigger gang of rogues. But it was under the rule of those rogues, not least occupying powers, like the Russians in Czechoslovakia, that the Word of God came to John, and had to be heard, worked out, lived out in the minute particulars of responsible love; in the terrifying decisions of when to speak and when to be silent, when to submit and when to be defiant, when to bow with the wind and when to give your body to be burned.

Motive: method: moment: minute particulars. And I'm going to add yet one word more—one more 'M'—which you may thing a strange bed-fellow with protest and violence, the word modesty. Oliver Cromwell, that great Protestant and Puritan witness, who was usually convinced he knew God's answer in any situation and indeed that he was God's answer, wrote in 1650, in a letter to the General Assembly of the Church of Scotland the memorable words: 'I beseech you in the bowels of Christ, think it possible you may be mistaken.' Now if I had been in that General Assembly I think I would have proposed sending the letter back with the words, 'And, dear Oliver, we beseech you in the bowels of Christ, think it possible you may be mistaken.'

Infallibility lies with Christ alone; not with the British, or the Russians, or the General Assembly of the Church of Scotland, or the Church of England, or the Church of Rome or with 'science'. 'Now we know in part, then shall we know even as we are known.' Therefore Christians have in their witness to be modest, though that sometimes may blunt the cutting edge of their witness. Now you cannot join a march of protest only half-believing in your cause. But it is not of half-hearted belief that I am speaking, but of the awareness that we haven't got all the truth. That awareness is part of the awareness of complexity which is part of mature Christian judgment. In South Africa, for instance, you can be aware that you haven't all the truth, but it would be lily-livered to treat apartheid as something towards which you can be apathetic.

So the motive of protest; the method of protest; the moment of protest; the minute particulars that are implied by your protest; the modesty of protest: all these are to be seen within the context and the perspective of Christ's love. But in my end is my beginning. Christian protest, witness, discipleship is affirmation at cost, at risk, grounded in the great and central truths of the Christian faith, and that means protest belongs not only to Opposition but to Government. And to have become a Christian is in my judgment to have committed oneself for life to what should be the greatest protest movement of all times.

CHAPTER TWENTY-ONE

THE UNITY OF THE CHURCH

by Cardinal JAN WILLEBRANDS,
Vatican Secretariat for Promoting Christian Unity

Let me first of all express my great joy and deep gratitude for the fact that at your gracious invitation I am able to join you before God in this prayer service to thank him and to beg of him full and complete unity in faith and love.

May I begin by quoting some words which you will not suspect of being taken from an ecumenical prayer or pamphlet:

... come with me you fools,
Into Unity of Holy Church—and hold we us there ...
And call we to all the commons—that they come unto Unity
and there abide and do battle—against Belial's children.

The blunt words are by the great prophetic poet of 14th-century England, Piers Plowman. They remind us that the unity of the Church, that effective sign of Christ living in her, is always a matter of urgency to visionary minds. The New Testament is full of this urgency; the fourth Gospel makes it the mark of the heirs of eternal life, of those who look with the eyes of faith beyond this world. It is the glory of those whom God has given to Christ his Son. 'Holy Father, keep them in thy name which thou hast given me, that they may be one even as we are one' (John 17:11 R.S.V.). He sent them into the world for the centuries to come and prayed 'for those who believe in me through their word, that they may all be one' (John 17:20-21 R.S.V.). If there is some glory in unity, in togetherness, in a bond of love, it is the glory of Christ, 'the glory which thou hast given me, I have given to them, that they may be one even as we are one' (John 17:22 R.S.V.). This glory, or, as the Greek expresses it *doxa*, marks the transcendence of God as it is appearing and manifesting itself to this world. This glory appears and manifests itself first of all in Christ, 'As thou, Father, art in me and I in thee,' but then also in us 'I in them' (John 17:23 R.S.V.) in so far as we remain united in him. Therefore, it is through that glory in unity that the world may know that Christ has been sent by the Father and that the love of the Father is in us. John the Evangelist, who is called also the Divine, is really the troubadour of love and unity. His Gospel and his first Letter are filled with this idea.

This unity is not only the inspired ideal of a troubadour. In the first record of Church history, the Acts of the Apostles, the primitive community of Jerusalem is described as gathered in the upper room 'with one accord devoted to prayer (Acts 1:14). St. Paul, in his Letter to the Romans, expresses his desire that they may 'live in such harmony with one another, in accord with Christ Jesus, that together you may with one voice glorify the God and Father of our Lord Jesus Christ' (Rom. 15:5–6 R.S.V.). St. Paul's wishes for the community in Rome are not merely a matter of local concern. In various ways he directs them to all the Christian Churches and communities. He tells the Corinthians, 'Because there is one loaf, we who are many are one body, for we all partake of the one loaf (1 Cor. 10:17 R.S.V.). To the Ephesians he speaks of the strength of unity, the integrity, candour and courage it brings to Christian witness. In his Letter to the Philippians, Paul has preserved for us the old Christian hymn on the divinity of Christ and the emptying of our Lord in the humility of the cross. This hymn, in which the primitive Christian community professed its faith, is introduced by Paul with the plea to 'complete my joy by being of the same mind, having the same love, being in full accord and of one mind' (Phil. 2:2 R.S.V.).

Now we all are conscious of the fact, and we confess it with repentance before God, that we have not preserved, in the obedience of faith, that unity through which we may all partake of the same bread, through which we should be in full accord and of one mind. However, we may thank God that humility and courage in the spirit of Christ have begun again to inspire the relations among Christians, among their Churches and communities. This new spirit has also been manifest in a particular way in the relations between the

Roman Catholic Church and the Anglican Communion during these recent years, years so charged with events of heavy import for Christianity.

For the Roman Catholic Church the second Vatican Council has been a great event for what it is contributing to theological reflection, to the renewal of the mission of the Church to the world of today, to the orientation it has given for relations with our Christian brethren of other Churches and Communities. From the very beginning, when he first announced the calling of an ecumenical Council, Pope John made it clear to the world that the restoration of Christian unity was one of his great hopes. Pope Paul, in his speech opening the second session, indicated the restoration of Christian unity as one of the main objectives of the Council.

In December 1960, after a pilgrimage to the Holy City of Jerusalem, Archbishop Fisher of Canterbury paid a visit to the Churches of Constantinople and Rome. For the first time since the Reformation, the Archbishop of Canterbury met the Pope. This fraternal encounter, in historical perspective so much more than a mere gesture of courtesy, was a stroke of vision pointing firmly towards the future. The Archbishops of Canterbury and York responded to the spirit and the words of Pope John and, already during the preparatory period of the second Vatican Council, sent a personal representative to Rome. The Archbishop of Canterbury, as the head of the Anglican Communion, led the way in accepting Pope John's invitation to send observers to the Council. When the Vatican Council turned to formulate Catholic principles on ecumenism and its practice, both Roman Catholics and Anglicans rejoiced that the Decree on Ecumenism spoke of the 'special place' held by the Anglican Communion 'among those in which some Catholic traditions and institutions continue to exist' (Decree on Ecumenism, No. 13).

Insight and a clear understanding of the many factors involved led Archbishop Ramsay to await the end of the Council's work before visiting Rome and the Pope. The Archbishop wanted to avoid giving any impression of wishing to influence the development of the discussions in the Council. Furthermore, he wished to give a firm basis to his visit by setting it within the context of the decisions already taken by the Vatican Council. The human warmth,

the spiritual elevation and the geniality of those days caught
the imagination of a world still sensing the movement of the
spirit over the waters. Whatever difficulties or setbacks may
arise from history or emotions, the spirit and the fruit of
the common prayer of the Pope and the Archbishop, as well
as the conviction and the faith expressed in their common
declaration, will remain a source and guiding principle for
the further development of our relations and will lead us to
that unity which is the object of our prayers and desires and
which is the promise and gift of the Lord to his Church.
The spiritual elevation and the geniality of the visit, pro-
longed so to speak in the life of the Anglican Centre founded
at that time in Rome, firmly established the tone of the
dialogue which Pope and Archbishop set in motion then.
It continues to shine through the earnest purpose of the
report which the Joint Preparatory Roman Catholic/Anglican
Commission made—a document full of hope, on which a
letter of the revered Cardinal Bea set the mark of Roman
Catholic approval, while the resolutions of the Lambeth Con-
ference showed how much it mirrored the aspirations of the
Anglican episcopate.

This very week the first fruits of these proposals are being
gathered: for six days a new Commission has seriously discussed the great issues on which, in appearance or reality,
we remain divided. But be sure that it has also discussed
what unites us—our resolve, under God, to accept the great
command of unity given by Christ and echoed in all the
writings of the New Testament, to accept also the great
challenge of Christian witness in this new age—a challenge
as broad and as deep as life itself. Some speak of this Commission as a 'permanent' commission. If the title were to
represent a forecast of the Commission's span of life, its
pessimistic outlook would frighten me, as I am sure it would
frighten the Commission members and yourselves. But this
is not the case. The title reflects rather the happy irreversi-
bility of the ways we have taken together.

What is the true meaning of these ways of dialogue?
Theological discussion is a necessary help to discover and
to manifest the unity in faith which we already enjoy and
to restore that unity where it has been lost. However, the
heart of the matter, I am sure, is what the Roman Catholic
Ecumenical Directory calls 'Communicatio in spiritualibus',

i.e. a share of spiritual activity and resources. The basis of this is our Christian brotherhood, securely grounded in the baptism by which we are reborn in Christ. Through this we turn confidently in prayer to the source of all that we hold good and true, drawing new things and old out of a deep, rich treasure. This treasure holds many things deriving from our common inheritance, many reflecting our particular genius and witnessing to the vitality of our particular history. Within the framework of such a sharing we need have no fear of candour and straight speech in theological discussions. We can be sure of blessing and ripeness in Christian co-operation which will increase and find many fields of practical application in local circumstances. This will be due to the fact that a solid basis of agreement in faith underlies such spiritual sharing and such common labour, as it provides the spur for that intense effort of prayer, of thought and imagination, that humble and courageous stretching of minds, which will in God's time discover, manifest and reintegrate unity in faith and give it its expression in Church unity.

None can deny that this unity in faith is indispensable; it is no less sure that diversity of theological approach and explanation is legitimate and can be acknowledged within the unity of faith, and within the Church. This important fact was expressed by Pope John in his address at the beginning of the Council: 'One thing is the deposit of faith, that is the truths preserved in our sacred doctrine, another thing is the way they are expressed while retaining the same meaning and substance.' This distinction has been reaffirmed by the Council itself (De Ecumenismo, No. 6).

Another important idea introduced by the Vatican Council, when it speaks of dialogue, was to acknowledge a 'hierarchy of truths': 'When comparing doctrines, theologians should remember that in Catholic teaching there exists an order or "hierarchy" of truths, since they vary in their relationship to the foundation of the Christian faith.' The importance of this idea has not escaped the theological world, but what it meant by the phrase is no less important. It does not mean that any part of revelation is less true than another, nor does it deny that we have to accept with the same act of faith all revealed truths. However, besides the formal aspect of revealed truths we have to consider also their content. In this respect religious truth is more important in proportion to its relationship to the foundation, or we may also say, to the Centre of Christian faith. In the explanation of this phrase given by the responsible conciliar commission, it was said: 'Truths upon which all Christians agree as well as truths in which they differ, should rather be weighed than counted' (*potius ponderentur quam numerentur*).

Without disparaging any truths, this principle gives a guide-line for every ecumenical dialogue and is of great importance and help for those who participate in theological dialogue. They carry a serious responsibility in their search for the manifestation and the restoration of unity. However, dialogue is not an end in itself: by remaining such, it becomes sterile. Accompanying work such as that done this past week at Windsor, there must be an enlargement, a process, an awakening of interest and aspiration, a sharing of spiritual activity and resources which always looks out towards the concerns of Christian mission and the challenge of the present age. Theological dialogue remains an indispensable service to arrive at this end. Dialogue on world level, inevitably tempted to great abstractions, is balanced by national and regional dialogue—in the U.S.A., in South Africa, Australia and elsewhere. For this balance to be realised we need full exchange of information between all these enterprises, and the authorities to whom their work is referred must face up to the task not only of passing on its benefits by various degrees of distribution and publication but also of integrating its results and aiding in their further developments.

If they work with this common mentality and are strengthened by God's grace, are obedient to our Lord's commands, and are enlightened by the Holy Spirit, might not our theologians then expect to see in the none too distant future, a vision of that unity in truth given us in Christ? I would go so far as to hope that a limited period, say five years, might allow them to give, conscientiously and loyally, this service they are qualified to give to the Churches. This would not mean that by that time we would have before us a full programme and concrete outline for a scheme of unity. Dialogue, however, would have entered upon a new stage, studying concrete ways and modalities of future unity. We would face then the challenge, most difficult yet most bracing of all—to explore what unity might mean in practice.

We should not feel tempted to imagine ourselves at the gates of the promised land—there is plenty of recent experience even of far advanced unity negotiations to moderate our euphoria—but rather than tempt us to superiority it would lead us to consolidation and to courage. Would it be courage or rashness to offer some further perspective, some pattern for the future?

May I invite you to reflect on a notion which, it seems to me, has received much fruitful attention from theologians recently? It is that of the *typos* in its sense of general form or character, and of a plurality of *typoi* within the communion of the one and only Church of Christ. When I speak here of a *typos* of the Church, I do not mean to describe the local or the particular Church in the sense the Vatican Council has given it. In the 'Decree on the Bishops' Pastoral Office in the Church' the Council describes the local Church or the diocese as 'that portion of God's people which is entrusted to a bishop to be shepherded by him with the co-operation of the presbytery. Adhering thus to its pastor and gathered together by him in the Holy Spirit through the Gospel and the Eucharist, this portion constitutes a particular church in which the one, holy, catholic and apostolic Church of Christ is truly present and operative.'

From this description it becomes clear that the local Church is not merely a part of the whole but that the fullness of the whole universal Church is present in the local Church, or if that fullness is not present in it, the local Church is not perfect and complete. Here we are not making a distinction between the essence of the Church and its empirical manifestation. The New Testament never makes this distinction when it speaks of Churches. We are talking about the universal Church which is manifest in a particular place. It is this meaning of the local Church which the Vatican Council has discovered again.

As distinct from this notion of the local Church, with all of the theological meaning it contains, the notion which I submit to your attention, that of a *typos* of a Church, does not primarily designate a diocese or a national Church (although in some cases it may more or less coincide with a national Church). It is a notion which has its own phenomenological aspects, with their particular theological meaning.

In the Decree on Ecumenism we read: 'For many centuries the Churches of East and West went their own ways, though a brotherly communion of faith and sacramental life bound them together' (No. 14). The theological element which must always be present and presupposed is the full 'communion of faith and sacramental life'. But the words 'went their own ways', point in the direction of the notion which I would like to develop a little more. What are these 'own ways' and when can we speak of a *typos*? A bit further on the Decree on Ecumenism explains that 'the heritage handed down by the apostles was received in different forms and ways, so that from the very beginnings of the Church it has had a varied development in various places, thanks to a similar variety of natural gifts and conditions of life' (No. 14).

Where there is a long coherent tradition, commanding men's love and loyalty, creating and sustaining a harmonious and organic whole of complementary elements, each of which supports and strengthens the other, you have the reality of a *typos*. Such complementary elements are many. A characteristic theological method and approach (historical perhaps in emphasis, concrete and mistrustful of abstraction) is one of them. It is one approach among others to the understanding of the single mystery, the single faith, the single Christ.

A characteristic liturgical expression is another. It has its own psychology; here a people's distinctive experience of the one divine Mystery will be manifest—in sobriety or in splendour, inclining to tradition or eager for experiment, national or supranational in flavour. The liturgical expression is perhaps a more decisive element because 'the liturgy is the summit towards which the activity of the Church is directed; at the same time it is the fountain from which all her power flows' (Const. on the Liturgy, No. 10).

A spiritual and devotional tradition draws from many springs—the Bible, the fathers, the monastic heritage, its own more recent classics. It meets new needs in its own way; its balance of joy and contrition, of action and contemplation, will be determined by history and temperament. A characteristic canonical discipline, the fruit also of experience and psychology, can be present. Through the combination of all of these, a *typos* can be specified.

In the Constitution on the Church of the second Vatican Council we read: 'By divine Providence it has come about that various Churches, established in various places by the apostles and their successors, have in the course of time coalesced into several groups, organically united, which, preserving the unity of faith and the unique divine constitution of the universal Church, enjoy their own discipline, their own liturgical usage, and their own theological and spiritual heritage' (No. 23). It is through such seated realities as these, and not because of mere territorial or national boundaries, that we can find the expression of a typology of Churches. Different *typoi* exist in countries where eastern and western Churches live together. If within one nation two *typoi* are so closely related, that in a situation of full communion between them, Providence draws them into coalescence, the authentic and strong elements of each will take their place in an enriched unity. Such a strengthening and enrichment will manifest itself primarily where it finds its highest motive—in a renewal of witness to Christ, a renewal of mission. A reunion which would not be a new Pentecost, a fresh manifestation of the eternal mystery to a time with its own spiritual needs, would be a nine days' wonder and little else.

It seems to me that Pope Gregory, in his famous letter to Augustine, archbishop of the English nation, opened the way for a new *typos* of the Church in western countries. He writes: 'My brother, you are familiar with the usage of the Roman Church, in which you were brought up. But if you have found customs, whether in the Roman, Gallican, or any other Churches that may be more acceptable to God, I wish you to make a careful selection of them, and teach the Church of the English, which is still young in the Faith, whatever you can profitably learn from the various Churches. For things should not be loved for the sake of places, but places for the sake of good things. Therefore select from each of the Churches whatever things are devout, religious, and right; and when you have arranged them into a unified rite, let the minds of the English grow accustomed to it' (Bede, *A History of the English Church and People*, I, 27, 2).

Obviously the very existence of different *typoi* 'added to external causes and to mutual failures of understanding and charity' can also 'set the stage for separations' (Decree on Ecumenism, No. 14). Through the grace of God, the ecumenical movement is creating understanding and charity and restoring unity between those who have grown asunder. The life of the Church needs a variety of *typoi* which would manifest the full catholic and apostolic character of the one and holy Church. If we are only going to fossilise, common sense would seem to suggest that it is not very important whether we do so together or separately. Unity is vital only if it is a vital unity.

None of us, I fancy, underestimates what is needed of wisdom and discernment, of strength and patience, of loyalty and flexibility, of forbearance, of willingness to teach and to learn, if we are to make progress towards this goal. Nor, happily, is any of us in doubt as to the sources whence we shall derive what we need. The movement we aspire to make together is within the one great dynamic, the *aedificatio Christi*. The tradition which is shared and enriched in a true typology is a living tradition—something which looks to the past only as it has vital meaning for the present and contributes dynamically to the future.

If a typology of Churches, a diversity in unity and unity in diversity, multiplies the possibilities of identifying and celebrating the presence of God in the world; if it brings nearer the hope of providing an imaginative framework within which Christian witness can transform human consciousness for today, then it has all the justification it needs.

For us, especially during this week of prayer for unity, there remains the call to perseverance, to a closer union of prayer in our common enterprise. St. Paul in his Letter to the Philippians has something to say to us here: 'So if there is any encouragement in Christ, any incentive of love, any participation in the Spirit, any affection and sympathy, complete my joy by being of the same mind, having the same love, being in full accord and of one mind' (Phil. 2: 1-2 R.S.V.).

CHAPTER TWENTY-TWO

NOTHING REALLY MATTERS

by the Bishop of Kingston, the Right Reverend HUGH
MONTEFIORE, formerly Vicar of Great St. Mary's

'Nothing really matters.' What an extraordinary text for
Whit Sunday, when we celebrate that great gale of the Spirit
which descended on to the small band of disciples, and
produced the Catholic Church which has spread throughout
the world! 'Nothing really matters'—but surely it *does*
matter and it has mattered and it will continue to matter.
Men and women will continue to hand on to others the good
news which they themselves have received, because it
matters. Men and women will continue to turn the world
upside down with Christian values precisely because the
world does matter and the world is worth trying to put right.
Listen to St. Peter on the first Whit Sunday as recounted
in the book of the Acts: 'Let all Israel then accept as certain
that God has made this Jesus, whom you crucified, both
Lord and Messiah.' That mattered. And listen again to the
response. 'Friends, what are we to do?' 'Repent', said Peter,
'repent and be baptised, every one of you, in the name of
Jesus the Messiah.' That mattered enough at any rate for
some three thousand souls to take action that very day.
   At first sight my text seems lunatically unchristian. And
certainly if you take it in the sense that none of us need do
anything ever about anything, then it is a thoroughly unchristian text, and I would not want to have anything else
to do with it. But that is not what is meant. The text is not
'Nothing matters' but 'Nothing really matters'. Let me try
to put the point another way. There is a saying, 'If a thing's
worth doing, it is worth doing well.' I expect that it is a
saying with which most of you would agree. It is certainly
one that I have tried—and of course failed—to put into practice. If our work is an offering to God, then we dare offer
him nothing but our best. Indeed is it not rather the case

that we want to offer him nothing but our best? You remember that lovely hymn of George Herbert:

> *All may of thee partake;*
> *Nothing can be so mean*
> *Which, with this tincture, For thy sake,*
> *'Will not grow bright and clean.*
>
> *A servant with this clause*
> *Makes drudgery divine;*
> *Who sweeps a room, as for thy laws,*
> *Makes that and the action fine.*

Drudgery remains drudgery. I think it's just pretending that drudgery can ever be anything else than drudgery. But when drudgery is an offering made to God, when it is as George Herbert puts it *for thy sake*, then if drudgery is worth doing, it is worth doing well.

And what is more, the demand of God upon each one of us is infinite. The sky is the limit. Christianity would never have spread the way it did if it made tepid claims and made lukewarm demands. On the contrary, there is no limit to what God demands of your life and mine. You have only to think back to the Gospels and see how the various sayings of Jesus drive home the limitless nature of those demands. 'What God has joined together, let no man put asunder.' 'You cannot serve God and money.' 'Unless your righteousness exceeds that of the scribes and the pharisees, you will never enter the kingdom of heaven.' 'Do not resist one that is evil. If anyone strikes you on the right cheek, turn to him the other one also.' And so one could go on and on. Jesus never pulled his punches. He made it quite clear that God's demand on us is unlimited, even if it means applying all these and his other sayings to various complex situations. But mere moral exhortation gets us nowhere. It is only frustrating. What we need is not so much being told what to do but the will and the inspiration and the staying power to do it. And it is precisely this that Whitsun commemorates —the will, the inspiration and the staying power to do it. The Holy Spirit of God that rested upon Jesus during his earthly life has been promised and given to his universal Church. It has been given to individual members and to the

Church as a whole to claim for themselves. We can call this gift grace if we like, we can speak of it as Christ in us, or we can call it the Holy Spirit. The name doesn't matter: it is the reality and the experience of the reality that has penetrated deep into men's hearts and turned their lives upside down and sent them out with faith, hope and charity to do God's work in the world.

But—and there is a but—this gift of the Spirit to us can make us feel very self-important. We can feel that God has delegated everything to us, that we are solely responsible for the world, and therefore we must not only do *our* best, we must also do *the* best that can be done. Now surely this should be questioned. This is first of all God's world and not ours. We are not solely responsible for the world, God bears the chief responsibility, and that includes the responsibility for making us weak and fallible human beings. There is a lovely prayer of Bishop Westcott which ends 'and when we have finished what thou hast given us to do, help us O Lord to leave the issue to thy wisdom'. We find this very difficult. We tend to worry and be anxious. Let me commend to you the prayer of Alcoholics Anonymous. I think it should be equally the prayer of Christians Anonymous. It goes like this:

> God grant me the serenity to accept the things I cannot change, the courage to change things I can, and the wisdom to know the difference.

The Holy Spirit of God does not and cannot alter our limitations: he can only fulfil our potentialities. And so perhaps I may put it in another epigram. If it is true that if a thing is worth doing it is worth doing well, it is also true that it is worth doing badly. This means that we can only do our best and we must be content with that; and our best may mean that we do something badly. It means too that it is worth aiming high and failing than never to aim at all. Browning put the point well in poetry:

> That low man seeks a little thing to do,
>   Sees it and does it;
> This high man, with a great thing to pursue,
>   Dies 'ere he knows it.

> *That low man goes on adding one to one,*
>   *His hundred's soon hit:*
> *This high man, aiming at a million,*
>   *Misses an unit.*
> *That, has the world here—should he need the next,*
>   *Let the world mind him!*
> *This, throws himself on God, and unperplext*
>   *Seeking shall find him.*

'A man's reach should exceed his grasp, or what's an heaven for?' We are given grace to face up to God's infinite demand, and we can do no more than our best; and if we feel that we could have done better (and often we do), then as Christians we feel not remorse, but rather happiness and freedom at the wonderful forgiveness of God. Put beside God in this way, nothing really matters.

Let me try to illustrate what I am trying to say in three ways; first, with reference to God, and secondly, with reference to the Church, and thirdly, with reference to ourselves. First, with reference to God, Sometimes we carry on as though God were dependent almost for his very existence upon the way we commend him to others. To take a contemporary illustration, John Allegro has written a book claiming that Jesus was really a cover-up for a society of Jewish drug addicts who fed themselves on a mushroom known as the fly agaric. I have discovered from the Professor of Botany at the Hebrew University in Jerusalem that this particular mushroom does not even grow in the Holy Land, but a little detail like this does not deter Allegro—he has not written that kind of book. Now I see that some mistaken Christians propose to sue Allegro for blasphemy under some ancient law of the kingdom. Quite apart from the fact that this will only make people the more eager to read this nonsense, it suggests that God needs us to look after him. But if he's really God, he doesn't. God doesn't need that kind of help. We must not be too self-important. God never leaves himself without witness. The Gospel of Jesus Christ is true, and truth does not need unworthy kinds of support. Of course we do our best to understand God, to respond to him, to witness to him. But compared to the transcendent majesty and power of God himself our own efforts, although we do the best we can, don't really matter.

And secondly, there's the Church. It is worth remembering that the first disciples did not decide that it was about time that the Holy Spirit was given to them and asked God for it. On the contrary, their experience on Whit Sunday was a colossal and unexpected surprise, the last thing that they or anyone else was expecting. The Holy Spirit is always the gift of God. Nowadays people get depressed because the visible Church is on the decline—and there is no doubt, statistically speaking, that it is on the decline. There are less babies baptised, less young people confirmed, less people take Holy Communion, less people attend church. Statistically the Churches are on the decrease, and it is a time of great change in matters of Christian belief and Christian behaviour and Christian worship. But if we get depressed by this, we forget the transcendance of God. Nothing really matters compared with God, not even the present-day Church. His Spirit is unpredictable. Do we not believe that the Holy Spirit can burst forth upon the Church as it did on the first Whit Sunday and has done many times since? Who would have believed that the moribund 18th-century Church of England could have possibly become the lively Church of the next century? Who could have believed that the empty college chapels of the 1930s, with only two or three in them, would become so crowded in the 1950s that people had to bring in extra chairs? We must not be too self-important about the part that we can play in the revival of the Church today. We must do our best, and leave it to God.

And lastly, there is ourselves. Let me remind you once again of the prayer of Alcoholics Anonymous:

God grant me the serenity to accept the things I cannot change, the courage to change things I can, and the wisdom to know the difference.

We tend to be anxious because we feel we have not done as well as we should have done. We tend to think that the little details of our own life are vastly important. Compared with God, nothing really matters. We do our best and leave it at that. Or, if we have not done our best (and that is often the case), we tell God we are sorry and will do better next time, and feel the Christian happiness of forgiveness. That is the right Christian attitude. But we tend to worry. We tend to feel remorse. Yet, in fact, compared with God, nothing really matters. How small and how petty are most of our personal worries, while as for our national and international anxieties, how little there is we can do! Examinations seem colossally important when you are preparing for them and often cause anxiety: but I would like to ask those of the congregation who took them twenty years ago—can you even remember the grades that you got? I remember as a very young curate upsetting the teapot over the table when the Bishop came to breakfast—and I remember his response, as the tablecloth rapidly changed colour. 'Now is the time to think of eternity,' he said. We could often repeat that to ourselves.

Today is Whit Sunday. We celebrate the coming of the Holy Spirit of God. It is a good day on which to take our attention off ourselves and give it to God, besides whom nothing really matters.